GW01607417

How did it feel?

The woman, twenty-five years old, screamed and shouted, rock & roll style. She'd been in high school when she first began to follow the words of Bob Dylan, and she'd been there the last time he played Chicago, in 1965. Now, as the man sang "The Times They Are A'Changin' " and, from his first album, his "Song to Woody," the woman seemed to be relearning her lines.

She turned to a friend, looking hopeful in the darkness and the marijuana mist. "It seems like it hasn't changed," she said. "It's the same kind of feeling."

Behind her a couple of rock freaks hung on the lyrics of "The Lonesome Death of Hattie Carroll." The first guy exulted: "Man, that song hit me," and his friend agreed: "Yeah, he got down!"

Later, the Chicago Stadium would burst into little flames, as many of the 18,500 first-nighters acclaimed "It's Alright, Ma (I'm Only Bleeding)" by striking matches, turning the hockey arena into a three-tiered crown of light....

KNOCKIN' ON DYLAN'S DOOR: On the Road in '74
is an original POCKET BOOK edition.

Knockin' on Dylan's Door

KNOCKIN' ON DYLAN'S DOOR

A Rolling Stone Book

MICHAEL DEMPSEY LONDON
IN ASSOCIATION WITH CASSELL & CO.

Michael Dempsey, in association with Cassell & Co.

35 Red Lion Square, London WC1R 4SG
Sydney, Auckland
Toronto, Johannesburg

First published in England 1975

I.S.B.N. 86018 104 9

Printed in Great Britain by R. J. Acford Ltd.,
Industrial Estate, Chichester, Sussex

Contents

The Press Reviews the Tour

Dylan Opens to a Hero's Welcome

By Ben Fong-Torres

The woman, 25 years old, screamed and shouted, rock & roll style. She'd been in high school when she first began to follow the words of Bob Dylan, and she'd been there the last time he played Chicago, in 1965. Now, as the man sang "The Times They Are A'Changin'" and, from his first album, his "Song to Woody," the woman seemed to be relearning her lines.

She turned to a friend, looking hopeful in the darkness and the marijuana mist. "It seems like it hasn't changed," she said. "It's the same kind of feeling."

Behind her a couple of rock freaks hung on the lyrics of "Lonesome Death of Hattie Carroll." The first guy exulted: "Man, that song hit me," and his friend agreed: "Yeah, he got down!"

Later, the Chicago Stadium would burst into little flames, as many of the 18,500 first-nighters acclaimed "It's Alright, Ma (I'm Only Bleeding)" by striking matches, turning the hockey arena into a three-tiered crown of light.

* * *

Bob Dylan, praise him, is back. On January 3rd, in the first winterlude of '74, he successfully kicked off his first tour since early 1966, when he completed the winter-long grind of a US and world tour and wrecked his neck in that motorcycle accident at Woodstock. By the time he finishes next month, he will have performed 40 concerts in 21 cities before a total of 658,000 people.

The tour, conceived last summer when Dylan and the Band got together in Malibu, the Southern California beach community, is more than what Dylan originally wanted: a chance to hit maybe a dozen cities, just to get out and play. Told by promoter Bill Graham that times had changed, that economic reality forbade short jaunts and that other realities made a small tour in front of small audiences impossible, Dylan agreed to a larger schedule, with ticket prices as high as $9.50 in some cities, bringing an expected gross of more than $5 million.

"I paid $30 for mine," said one young man after the first Chicago concert, "and it was worth it. I was offered $50 for it, and I'm glad I didn't sell it."

"I've waited six, seven years for this," said another fan, who paid $9.50 and had no complaints.

For the money, they got one of numerous versions of the Dylan/Band show. Out of Malibu came enough songs—80, in fact, according to one close friend—"to do a different show—a different mix of songs—every night."

Chicago saw a moving, 2½-hour show, carefully planned—if not yet rehearsed down pat—to show off the Band as more than Dylan's backup, as it was in 1965, 1966 and at the Isle of Wight in 1969, and to show Dylan as a healthy, confident man at ease with all the identities and roles he has created and that have surrounded and sometimes saddled him over the years: protest voice, radical poet, absurdist folk-rocker, romantic loser, country gentleman, family man.

But Dylan, still refusing to play any role, did all the songs—folk, rock, country and pop—in one shockingly strong voice, the songs mostly rearranged into what might best be called basic Band rock, searing and soaring, unified and precise, on a bedrock of backwoods America. Excellent in itself; perfect as a support for Bob Dylan.

The careful planning has Dylan and the Band all together for an hour (therefore saving the Band the task of being the opening act, the stall before the arrival of a god), then Dylan by himself, the Band by itself and a group finale. Sound thinking and a full show. But a sample of reactions after the concert indicated a clear desire for more Dylan, less Band. As one woman put it: "Who came to see the Band?" No matter their quality, they were seen —and preferred—as backup.

On opening night, the first discovery for the audience was an attempted coziness on the stage, through props reminding one of Neil Young, Martin Mull and an Uncle Sol furniture sale. There wasn't just a rug, some candles, a sofa and a coat rack, but also a Tiffany-style table lamp, a roll-top desk, an antique rocking chair, a set of conga drums, a bunk bed with frumpy blue mattresses, a multicolored wood chest housing a fire extinguisher and, at the bottom of the stage steps, a mat reminding the stars to WIPE YOUR FEET.

Dylan came out wrapped in a gray muffler, as if direct from the 13-degree weather. He wore a short black suede jacket, with a white shirt hanging out underneath, and blue jeans. He had an almost-growth of beard. His harpbrace was strapped into place, around the neck. He picked his way between the amps and the antiques and picked up his guitar. He said nothing as he received the first of numerous standing ovations, just strummed his electric guitar as the group moved into a rocking "Hero Blues," a little-known, on-the-highway song from the early days.

Dylan seemed edgy, staring out to a fixed spot in the rear of the arena, but he was easy in his stage movements, bending his knees with the beat, swaying easily, slowly, back from the mike between lines. The voice was reminiscent of *Highway 61,* the transitional rock voice, with less of the harshness, more of the confidence.

On "Lay Lady Lay," Dylan dropped the Nashville affectations, the country-boy softness, stretching out last words of lines, snapping them off, talk-singing notes. Now he seemed more aware that he was on a stage again. He assumed an early Elvis stance, legs wide apart, firmly planted, guitar diagonal. After a third number—from the new Dylan/Band album—the Band rolled into "The Night They Drove Old Dixie Down," Levon Helm singing from behind the drums, Dylan facing him, his back turned to the audience, just a sideman. Rick Danko did "Stage Fright," with Robbie Robertson, shaven and looking like a better-fed Stevie Winwood, playing a weeping, sweeping lead while Dylan held down the rhythm.

Dylan then sang "It Ain't Me Babe," going back to a nine-year-old album, *Another Side of Bob Dylan,* doing the song more slowly, with a more pronounced beat, holding his guitar against his side, like a rifleman, for the second verse. The Band excelled, with Danko, Robertson and Helm taking turns on the fills. "Leopard Skin Pillbox Hat," circa '66, was done circa '74, humor intact.

Richard Manuel did "Share Your Love," with Dylan doing the fills on harp, and then it was "All Along the Watchtower," from *John Wesley Harding,* Dylan, crouching, animated, earning his third standing ovation for this, his third look back. On opening night he did songs from all his albums except *Freewheelin', Self-Portrait* and *New Morning.*

Dylan appeared, after a Band number, with shades, took the piano for "Ballad of a Thin Man," and went back on guitar for "I Don't Believe You," pausing after the first line and accelerating the Band to match his mood: super-sneering, whipping out each line at this woman he seemed to be remembering so well from 1964. Another ovation, and funny, for this was the song that had drawn paper plates, cups and boos in August, 1965, at Forest Hills, New York, Dylan's first concert after the disaster at Newport Folk. With him in his then-new half-acoustic, half-rock show: Robbie and Levon.

Dylan addressed the audience for the first time. "Back in 15 minutes," he revealed, and the group left.

At intermission, Al Aronowitz, the New York pop critic and long-time friend to Dylan and the Band, glowed and gloated. Among the four Chicago papers, his piece alone predicted an outright Dylan triumph. Others asked, "Can he do it?"—that is, live up to the various roles—and expressed hope, but with a touch of depression, at the thought of a man having to try and live up to a legend. Aronowitz, in whose house Dylan had written "Mr. Tambourine Man," called Bob a heavyweight with a career "just beginning," who had not deteriorated a bit. Now, as if he knew, he promised: "You ain't seen nothing yet."

He knew. Dylan returned by himself with acoustic guitar, in a white shirt-jacket, and, after a momentary bout of slurring over forgotten words, ripped through "The Times They Are A-Changin'." Suddenly, clearly, we heard the old Dylan, sensed the old charisma, felt the old charge. He softened up for "Song to Woody" ("The world seems sick and hungry, tired and torn. It looks like it's a-dying and it's hardly been born").

The audience was getting a lesson. Dylan could still sing the "message" songs, and, like the best of poetry, they were proving timeless. "Lonesome Death of Hattie Carroll," about the lawlessness of power in Maryland, hit hard, post-Agnew. Dylan went soft again with a love song for wife Sara, the only woman he'd try for, to live and die for; the only one who doesn't try to tell him or sell him anything. From there he hit a high point: "It's Alright, Ma," the crowd exploding after the lines: "Goodness hides behind its gates but even the President of the United States sometimes must have to stand naked." The reading was powerful, the feeling, again, deja vu, the people responding, once more, as if one song, one singer, could make a difference. Dylan left the stage to the Band.

Robertson, Helm, Danko, Manuel and Garth Hudson huddled for a moment, while the three-minute ovation roared on over them. They finally broke out into "Life Is a Carnival," "The Shape I'm In," "When You Awake" and a ragged "Rag Mama Rag." Some people noticed the show of strength, the show of versatility and unity in an impossible situation. But it was an impossible situation, all the careful planning now in vain, as perhaps the best rock group in the country tried to follow Dylan's overwhelming, most compelling performance in too many years.

Dylan returned, the Band staying, and surprised again with a love song, a gentle communication to the audience, opening with the line: "May God bless and keep you always," and repeating the greeting: "May you stay far-ever young. . . ."

Finally, in answer to evening-long requests, Dylan came up with another peak: "Like a Rolling Stone," the Band matching Dylan's every ringing sting. "Rolling Stone" was the 25th number of the night. The Band did one more, "The Weight," as an encore, and Dylan closed the night on a lighter note: "Most Likely You Go Your Way (I'll Go Mine)" and left to a final, loving, five-minute ovation.

He had done it: satisfied the younger listeners, who dominated the audience, with rock & roll and a primer of early Dylan, and moved the older followers with a taste of what he had been and, at least for the moment, could be once again.

(In the second show, changes were made. Dylan, with the Band as backup, did six songs in a row, including "Just Like Tom Thumb's Blues" and his classical/rock piano performance on "The Ballad of a Thin Man." The Band then did a set of their own, six familiar tunes including "Long Black Veil" and "I Shall Be Released." Dylan returned for three more with the Band, including "Knockin' on Heaven's Door." His solo spot was followed by four more strong Band numbers, and for an encore he rocked "Maggie's Farm." Again, a peaceful, attentive audience. Again, Dylan's determined, businesslike silence between songs—except a "Don't go away" at intermission and a handshake with a front-row fan at the very end.)

Backstage Bill Graham pulled a cigar out of his mouth, an expensive model, $9 the box. "It's my second one," he said. "Eight to go." A cigar for every show. Or, as Graham put it, "It's a new baby every night."

"The Chicago date will be the shakedown date, almost like a rehearsal date," David Geffen had said. Geffen is the 30-year-old ex-mailroom boy at William Morris who became a manager of pop superstars. Now, he's chairman of Elektra/Asylum Records, and he signs and records them. On the evening before the first show, he, Dylan and the Band—no wives, women or families—had stepped off the Starship One, the 40-passenger 707 that's been refurbished, rock-star style (bedrooms and lounges, bar and gourmet foods, video cassette system and electric piano). The aircraft is rented out to the likes of Led Zeppelin, Elton John, the Stones and, now, Dylan, at $5 the mile, $20,000 for a coast-to-coast round trip. For a big group, reasonable. For seven. . . .

"Well," said Geffen, "frankly it was a mistake. We just didn't know how many people were actually coming." Geffen was calling to fill some of the Dylan information vacuum, to field rumors, answer questions, announce the latest Dylan changes.

For one, he said, Dylan has given up the idea of having his own record label and is now signed to Asylum. "He'll still do other projects—artists he finds he may want to help out. He'll just get them onto Asylum." Why the change? "He just changes. He just decided he no longer wanted a label. 'There are enough labels in this world.' That's what he said."

The album recorded with the Band is delayed two weeks, Geffen added, until January 17th. Also, there's a new title: *Planet Waves*. The delay, Geffen said, was due to the album cover, a painting by Dylan, "not being ready yet."

Dylan and the Band rehearsed in Los Angeles for two days—December 26th and 27th—at the Forum, where they will end the tour February 14th. The Forum, with 19,000 capacity, is just about the right size for rehearsals. Still, when the group reached Chicago, they weren't quite ready. The sound system, said Geffen, was wrong at the rehearsals, and an early morning sound check took place at the Chicago Stadium. The crew had laid out stage and light plans the afternoon before. Now, on concert day, at 2:45 PM, the musicians gathered together once more for a run-through. Two hours later, having gone over everything but the Dylan solo spot, they felt ready.

Chicago, actress Sarah Bernhardt said, is "the pulse of America." A burgeoning, changing city with a background of Al Capone and South Side blues, Chicago today, on the eve of the return of Bob Dylan, was paranoia, ignorance and small-time, small-town fanaticism.

The paranoia was in the papers—864 murders in 1973, second only to New York, twice Chicago's population; more killings than in four years of war in Northern Ireland, the paper said. It was in the cab driver's route, as he bypassed the Division Street offramp in fear of a nearby black housing project. "They take potshots at you," said the bearded young hack. There had been sniping incidents reported in the Cabrini Green projects; two "community relations" cops had been shot and killed.

As for Dylan: "Dylan? You mean Bobby? He's in town? I didn't know. But then, I don't read the papers." Still, as he gave walking directions to a midtown hi-fi shop, he suggested walking one way but cabbing another. Potshots.

The papers heard the word about Dylan through a local gossip column, then waited, like most people, for the December 2nd announcement. They dutifully reported the response: 37,000 tickets gone in two days, "thousands of requests unfilled." And yet, when three weeks later the stadium found a way to squeeze in another 500 at each show (the sound and light crew didn't need as much room as they thought they would), no one thought to advertise, and no one thought to offer them to those who'd missed out on the first 37,000. Only a last-minute announcement brought the ticket-buyers to the box office, some as late as the day of the concert. (Bill Graham even announced the availability of the second 500 seats at the end of the first show.)

In the weeks before the concert, the newspapers' coverage of the coming event conveyed little sense of excitement. Reporters grumbled about the location of the stadium: "You have to go past the wino district to get there," said one. "It's in this depressed black shit area, where it seems that there are rifle scopes looking down on you."

An alternative spot might have been the Arie Crown Theater. But it was ruled out. "Chicago," said Geffen, "is one of the three largest cities, and it seemed unfair to play to just 8000."

The last time Dylan played Chicago, in 1965, he played the Arie Crown. "That's when he was doing that half-hour show," said a woman who saw him there and, later, in Miami. "The purists booed him in the rock part. But not as bad as Forest Hills." Since '65 the Arie Crown has burned to the ground and been rebuilt.

Dylan had been to Chicago two other times: Once, in 1960—exactly 14 years ago, in fact—he stayed several weeks on the way, he was saying, to New York and to visit Woody Guthrie in Jersey. He wrote the city off as "dirty, smelling," wrote his "Song to Woody" here, and played guitar at one of the girls' dorms at the University of Chicago.

And in 1964, with his performance fee up to around $100 a week, he did two nights at a short-lived, step-down, uptown folk and jazz spot called The Bear, for free. The owner was broke, and Dylan wanted the exposure. Today, The Bear is gone. The house that stood above it, considered haunted by many of its tenants, was razed and replaced by an Enco gasoline station.

This time Dylan came into town wanting anything but exposure. David Geffen ran down the turndowns: cover stories in "all the big magazines" including *Paris Match* and *Der Spiegel;* an hour-long Cronkite news special for CBS; a $3 million guarantee to let a major studio do a feature film of the tour; a $100,000 guarantee to sell buttons in the lobby, and "at least a dozen books." All together, Bill Graham said, the tour had received ticket requests amounting to $92 million via 5.5 million pieces of mail in 21 cities.

Dylan's reaction to it all, said Geffen, is "kind of amazed. He's flattered and he would've liked for more people to be able to see him." So he may tour again? "I frankly doubt it."

But one thing was certain, Geffen maintained: "He's not going to cater or pander to the media. He feels it's nothing more than a concert tour. He considers himself, still, a songwriter, period."

Bullshit.

"Well," Geffen conceded, "he's not being realistic. But then, he doesn't have to be realistic. I mean, he knows he's a big star, but all he knows is that every time he sees his name in print, there's some weirdness with it. At least if he says nothing, people won't misquote him."

At best the thinking is simplistic, and, in fact, by the day of the second concert things had loosened up considerably at Dylan's hotel. He chatted with one reporter from a news magazine in the morning; then, lounging around that afternoon, obviously at ease, asked another reporter about the audience—what the age range was. Told that some critics and fans had expressed disappointment that he hadn't done more of a solo spot, he shrugged: "Well, you can't have everything." But, he said, he'd add the reporter's suggestion, "Love Minus Zero—No Limit." And he did. He also hinted at what did happen that night: A re-ordering of his set with the Band. As for the choice of "Hero Blues" as an opener, Dylan smiled: "Gotcha, huh?" In case you thought there was some *significance* to be found in the lyric or in the choice of the song as an opener.

Over the hotel phone, at two in the morning, Geffen summed it up: "This particular event," he said, "has drawn more response from the people than any event in media, bigger than Woodstock, Watkins Glen, any of those. You know, the Japanese chartered a *jet* here. A whole jetful of people, and I don't know how they could've gotten tickets, and now I've gotta go to radio stations and scrounge up tickets for them. I mean, they chartered a *plane* to get over here. I can't not give them tickets."

Who else, we asked, has asked him for tickets? "All the Beatles, the Kennedys, the Rockefellers, Mayor Lindsay."

The Kennedys wanted a dozen tickets. Will they get them?

"Well, now," Geffen laughed. "You can't turn down the Kennedys!"

Knockin' on Dylan's Door

By Ben Fong-Torres

We are in Toronto, the third stop of the Bob Dylan tour. Locked in by snow and still locked out, so far, from the inner circles of Dylan and the Band, I'm reduced to television in my hotel room. I choose Channel 6 and get 79, where a newsy-talk program called *The CITY Show,* named after the station's call letters, is on. For some reason, the moderator, a sporty-looking fellow, 50 or so, looks familiar, but the camera cuts to the program's "youth reporter," whose report this evening is an earnest attack on Dylan, the tour and tour producer Bill Graham. He is asking where all the money is going; he is characterizing Dylan as a "manipulator" of his fans and the press, secreting himself from the public after that convenient little bike spill and, now, exploiting his absence from the scene. He also has heard that Dylan's show is comprised mostly of older songs, and this, too, is a pisser for him.

The moderator, the man with those penetrating, close-set eyes I've seen before, comes to Dylan's defense:

"I believe there's a freedom to just sit down if you

want to," he tells the kid. "The public doesn't own Dylan; that's why he appealed to you in the first place.

"There's something sad about it: It's like Hemingway writing one book and the audience reading it over and over again and wanting nothing else."

As for Dylan's manipulation of the media, he continues, "You know I don't like to talk about my son too much on the air, but Neil has found that he's not dependent on all this damned media coverage." (Now I recognized the gentleman: Scott Young, Neil's father and a newspaper columnist in Toronto.) He goes on: "Just a line in the papers is enough. I've seen in Neil two different aspects. One is the concert, where he doesn't have to do anything —show up and they're pleased. The other is, he has a film out now, and it's not a successful one. Warner Bros. decided not to release it, and now he owns it. We talked about it; he talked about bringing it to Toronto. I told him, if you've got something to sell, and people are clamoring for it, sell it.

"Dylan is trying," he concludes, "to reestablish that there still is a Dylan around."

The next night, I met Dylan, bumping into him in the hallway up on his floor, and he agreed to talk—later, in Montreal. Three days later, in Montreal, 33 floors up at the Chateau Champlain, Bob Dylan sat across the table, at ease, in white western shirt and jeans, still sleepy at 3 PM, but willing to talk.

He's always interested in what his audience is thinking, so I told him about the impression his new love songs seemed to be making. Critics—from Chicago through Philadelphia and Canada—were saying he'd mellowed out, "blunted his image," "drained the venom from his voice." He'd moved from urgent, surging metaphorical poetry to clinch-cliches, stereotyped images, and an emphatically stated need for his loved one, a complete turnaway from his previous posture of independence, individualism and defiance.

Of course, he's played with such talk before. In "I'll Be Your Baby Tonight," he rhymed "moon" and "spoon." In Montreal, just last night, between "Don't Think Twice, It's

All Right" and "Gates of Eden," he told the audience: "That was a love song, and this one's another love song."

With a wife and five children, Dylan is being called a family man, or, as Jonathan Takiff, pop critic for the *Philadelphia Daily News* put it, "a dutch uncle."

"Yeah," said Dylan. "But those things don't make a person settle down. A family brings the world together. You can see it's all one. It paints a better picture than being with a chick and traveling all over the world. Or hanging out all night.

"But," he maintained, "I still get that spark. I'm still out there. In no way am I not. I don't live on a pedestal.

"Fame threw me for a loop at first," Dylan continued. "I learned how to swim with it and turn it around—so you can just throw it in the closet and pick it up when you need it."

The turning point, he said, was in Woodstock, "a little after the accident. There I was, sitting one night under a full moon, I looked out into the bleak woods and said, 'Something's gotta change.' There was some business that had to be taken care of, that we don't have to go into." I nodded, not mentioning the breakup with manager Albert Grossman, but reminding him of the problems he'd had fulfilling contracts for a book and a TV special.

"It was too much," he said. "It finally broke the camel's back. Now it's the same old me again."

Whatever that may be.

One of the reasons for following Dylan around, even if ultimately you learn that he's just the same old him, is that so many people are looking for so much from the drifter's return—for some kind of statement, either from the mere act of his reemergence or from something that a "new" Dylan may have to say. But too many of those that are filling up the papers and the airwaves with their Dylanalyses never heard, really *heard,* the man in the first place, or refused to accept what they were told: "It's not to stand naked under unknowing eyes/It's for myself and my friends my stories are sung," he sang, in "Restless Farewell," even before "My Back Pages."

Dylan says he's touring only because he wants to play

his music for the people. But the people, the papers say, want more than music. They want The Word.

"I don't understand that attitude," says Robbie Robertson of the Band. "I don't ever remember him ever delivering what they believed he delivered, or what they think he's going to deliver now. I mean, I heard a lot of terrific lines and songs. He certainly had a way of saying something that everybody felt, a way of phrasing it and condensing it down. But people have a fictitious past in mind about him."

I agreed. But even if I, for one, never saw Dylan as a messiah, idol, prophet, leader, or even a particularly great singer, I must admit, as have other journalists (whose style it is to not confess such things) that Dylan has touched me. And the nerve that was hit ties somehow back to the Sixties. During the second show in the Chicago Stadium, near the end of "It's Alright, Ma (I'm Only Bleeding)," it hit. It wasn't the song, a simple enough affair over an even simpler acoustic guitar run, that did it. For me, Dylan made a statement through a tone he was painting with his bitter-truth voice, a feeling of knowing resignation, the uplift deriving from the knowledge that here was a guy who'd seen it all, saw through it all, and . . . well, had a way of phrasing it, of condensing it down.

I watched this still-small, still-vulnerable figure, behind his guitar, looking up and bawling, "I got *nothing,* Ma, to live up to," and I shivered and thought of my older brother Barry, a probation officer and community worker murdered in the summer of 1972, in the midst of the gang wars of Chinatown. He left a mother and father who cannot stop mourning, and when "It's Alright, Ma" pulsed through the verse:

> While them that defend what they cannot see
> With a killer's pride, security
> It blows the mind most bitterly
> For them that think death's honesty
> Won't fall upon them naturally
> Life sometimes
> Must get lonely

I found myself wiping away tears with an index finger and thinking something toward Barry, something excusably maudlin like: "Can you see? Bob Dylan, someone you heard and liked a lot, is here."

Later, talking with reporters from *The New York Times* and the *Los Angeles Times,* I learned that they, too, had had the chills. And in the next city, Jon Takiff—"Philadelphia's Mr. Cynical," the publicist for the Spectrum rock auditorium called him—would walk away from the press box and tell me that "Like a Rolling Stone" had made him cry. And all the lofty articles I'd read about Dylan, all the burdensome books, suddenly meant very little. I'd have to meet the guy for myself.

Phil Ochs was in Philadelphia the day Dylan arrived. Ochs had a gig at the Main Point, a small club in suburban Bryn Mawr. Ochs used to hang out with Dylan, wanted to be as big as Dylan, admired Dylan's successful switch to rock, and served as a target for Dylan's celebrated personal attacks on Village friends. The most popular of the incidents had Ochs getting thrown out of Dylan's limousine one day, for not thinking "Can You Please Crawl Out Your Window" would be a smash.

The Main Point had no one answering its phone when I called, but a Dylan tour spokesman assured me that Phil and Bob had made up; that Ochs had even been invited to one of the concerts.

And scheduled to follow Ochs: John Hammond, Jr., who almost exactly ten years ago had found the Hawks in Toronto and brought them to the attention of Dylan. And opening for Hammond would be Leon Redbone, a mysterious folk and blues figure I'd be hearing about in Toronto, and from a Redbone fan named Dylan.

By Philadelphia, Dylan and the Band had their show pretty well set. The cluttered-attic look of the Chicago shows had been modified; Dylan and the Band came out strong, with six straight Dylan songs, concluding with Dylan cool-jerking the piano for "Ballad of a Thin Man," followed by six Band tunes. Dylan returned for three more, finished up with "Knockin' on Heaven's Door." An intermission of exactly 15 minutes was broken by Dylan's return as a solo acoustic artist for about five numbers, ending with "It's Alright, Ma." The Band came back for three or four more, finishing up with "The Weight" from *Big Pink,* and Dylan returned with a couple of newer songs, from *Planet Waves,* and the finale, "Like a Rolling Stone." And the encore was "Most Likely You Go Your Way (I'll Go Mine)."

In Toronto, Dylan began to open and close the shows with "You Go Your Way." Dylan explained, simply: "It completes a circle in some way."

By Philadelphia, the sound and light crews were in control of each show. Eighteen men were on the road for this one, under employment by Bill Graham's FM Productions. It was Graham and tour coordinator Barry Imhoff who came up with the living-room furniture for the stage; it was Graham ordering the house lights up on "Like a Rolling Stone." Now, he's huddling with lighting manager Bruce Byall, while the third-show crowd is still clearing the Spectrum.

Byall sits behind a board, 22 rows back on the main floor, and directs the constantly changing, carefully choreoraphed lighting.

Graham has by now heard "It's Alright, Ma" five times, and each time "Even the President of the United States sometimes must have to stand naked" gets the biggest reaction of any line in the concert.

"Tell you what I'd like to try," says Graham. "When Bob hits that line, how about switching to reds from overhead"—Graham sweeps a huge left arm out and down—"blues from the sides, and white spotlights directly onto him." Bruce agrees to give it a try. And as corny as the idea may sound, it'll work, the colors spread out far enough apart to be subtle. It is not, to be sure, a United States flag lit up by a thousand light bulbs.

But Toronto, the next stop, greets the effect, and the line, even, with more detached amusement than determined agreement. Michael McClure has joined the tour now; together we will go after his old friend Bob Dylan. McClure is uncomfortable; in the snow-sludge-slop-shuffle outside, he has lost his scarf, without which his neck is incomplete; he is seated just below the bank of speakers perched atop a tower at one corner of the stage, and he's got his ears finger-plugged to balance out the insistent highs. But he can still smell—"They're smoking rubber marijuana here," he says—and he can see. "You see how much *cleaner* these kids are?" No, I don't. The poet/playwright picks out a row of three boys in Pendleton shirts. They are indeed clean shirts. "See? Canada hasn't been fucked over by the War Machine!"

McClure asks me to ask three young men, in the row in front of us, why they've got their yarmulkes bobby-pinned on—"Ask them if they always wear them to rock concerts." I do, and get a glare. "It's personal," said one of them. "Ask them if they always smoke dope in their yarmulkes," said McClure, but I was busy concentrating on the music.

The Toronto audience is as respectful of Dylan as the States crowds, but even more attentive. There's less of the screaming for requests during pauses between numbers; less of the demands for Dylan while the Band is doing one of their own sets. But of course, this is Band territory. CHUM, the FM rock station, even embraces Dylan, referring to him as being "from Hibbing, Minnesota, very close to the Canadian border." Dylan himself, later, will admit a special feeling for Canada that gets him smiling a crack more onstage, gets him saying, twice in one show, "Great to be back in Montreal!" and singing a particularly strong and croony version of "Girl From the North Country." Dylan, later, will explain, looking out the wall-wide arched window in his hotel room, out beyond the office buildings, into the bleak woods: "Canada seems to bridge a gap between the United States and Europe. It's a certain flair. And this is where I come from, this kind of setting—lakes, and boats and bridges."

In Toronto, before the first of the two shows there, I call on CHUM and find a Dylan freak named John Donebie, who remembers that Dylan's been in town three times before, twice as a solo artist, around '62 and '63, and, in 1966, with the Hawks, who got huffily dismissed by one local critic as "a third-rate Toronto rock & roll band." In fact, the Hawks—and it's well-known—came up as the backup band for Ronnie Hawkins, the Arkansas rockabilly singer who'd moved to Canada in 1960. (His hits were in '59—"Forty Days" and "Mary Lou.") The Hawks, all from Canada, except drummer/Arkansas native Levon Helm, got tired of the roads they traveled, mostly in Southern states and along a short stretch of drink joints on Yonge Street in Toronto. Away from Hawkins, they continued to work Canada, were found by Hammond, sat in with him on a couple of albums, and met Dylan.

"You know," said Donebie, "Hawkins is still playing at the Nickelodeon down on Yonge Street. He's always there —or whenever he wants to play there, anyway. Just about owns the place. You ought to check him out." I make a note, and, after the first show (My notes remind me: "Overall feel of concert is LAZY"), I call the club. Ronnie is right by the phone and will be happy to see ROLLING STONE, spill some beer and stories, and, "Hey, Levon said he might come down tonight."

The Nickelodeon is an eat-drink-and-dance place, with pizza tablecloths, red flowery paper lamps, and a required coat check, just like in all the fancy restaurants in town. It feels like a hustlers' hall, a singles spot where, if you don't score, there's always Jingles upstairs, where you can take pictures of guaranteed naked ladies.

At the club, in a cluttered storage room full of discarded chairs, Hawkins was as hearty and jovial as ever. He's still cutting records, he said, two a year for Monument, but he hasn't had a record big enough to pay for a tour. He mostly stays fixed here, six nights a week, five sets a night —except when his boys are in town.

"I was over at the hotel last night and we brought back memories for seven hours," he said. And he saw the show tonight—"first time I've seen 'em play since they left in 1965"—and paid due compliments.

"They were always two years ahead of their time. Robbie was the first guy to get into white funk, in Canada or anywhere." Hawkins urged me to stay, see if Levon shows up.

Minutes later, at 12:30, an hour and a half since the end of the Dylan concert, the Nickelodeon broke into applause and cheers. Levon, and Robbie Robertson, and Rick Danko, and Bob Dylan, and friends, had passed the checkroom, all their coats, fur caps and mufflers intact. It was a nice little 39th-birthday present for Hawkins, and he leapt through the crowd to exchange warm greetings with Dylan, who wore shades and would stay mostly quiet through the night.

Hawkins jumped onto the stage with his latest congregation—a six-piece outfit that had Bill Graham nodding favorably—and told the buzzing crowd: "They came all the way from L.A. to hear me sing 'Forty Days!' " One of the waiters slapped his open hand, softly, repeatedly, against a counter. "Goddamn," he said to another worker. "Bob Dylan. Bob Dylan."

Hawkins introduced a special number. "I remember Robbie called it one of Bob's best songs at one time," he said, and moved into a mellow country version of "One Too Many Mornings," one of Dylan's earlier true-love songs, from 1964. A couple of birthday dedications later, Hawkins was rolling through "Bo Diddley" and worked in a couple of verses of "The Ballad of Hollis Brown." Dylan nodded and smiled.

After Hawkins' set, the crowd was quiet, a nickelodeon full of Dylan-watchers, picture-snappers. I got a good close-up look at him, for the first time, and he looked tired, in no shape to be club-nobbing, but not unapproachable. Later, at two o'clock, while the club tried to kick everybody out, Graham looked to be trying to set up a private jam session, talking soothingly to the people in charge. But they didn't go for it, and Graham resigned himself to the usual: a spread of food and wine on the artists' floor at the hotel.

Bob Dylan has had reason to avoid ROLLING STONE; we'd been among the most critical about his recent albums; the most cynical about his motives for the tour, launched in combination with a new label deal and a new album. He didn't need the media, didn't want to do interviews, all reporters were told. And that word seemed to have spread effectively around the tour. In Toronto, one writer spent 18 column-inches describing how he chased the Band's equipment van from the Malton Airport halfway across town, at a sometimes furious, speed-of-*Bullitt* pace before giving up. And at the Inn on the Park, before the first concert, another reporter spotted Dylan, in shades, at the hotel newsstand, leafing through a pube magazine called *Success*. Dylan denied that he was Dylan, but let a photographer take pictures. The reporter hit him up again, and Dylan, exasperated, told him, "Look, man, I'm not him." Finally, a friend came and helped him escape.

Still, his most intimate protectors insisted, Dylan would be happy to have a chat—if you happened to run into him. Now, Graham invited us to join the post-concert nibbling and listening-to-the-new-album gathering, and at 2:30 AM, I entered the most boring hotel suite I'd seen since my own Holiday Inn room back in Philadelphia. McClure and Byall were having a chat on one couch; Barry Imhoff was eating a plateful of snacks, and a lone teenaged girl wandered around wondering what she was doing.

But soon enough, there was a burst of noise from the hallway and a gang of Band members and buddies were scurrying past, followed by Bob Dylan, still in shades. He made a turn toward the party room, stopped in front of me, and continued to yell, half-puzzled, half-joking, after the little mob.

My moment had come. I introduced myself, and he kept his smile on as we shook hands. His was cold, offered downward, with not much of a grip. Then he excused himself, but promised, without my asking, "I'll be right back and we'll talk." Ten minutes later, at 3 AM, we sat side-by-side on couches and talked; he'd read some of my stories; I'd heard some of his songs.

We chatted, in idle, for maybe ten minutes . . . "How'd you like the show?" . . . "Well, you see, I wasn't feeling that great, I just had a flu shot today" . . . "No, 18,000 people yelling isn't that much of a thing. It's nothing new.

See, I used to sit in the dark and dream about it, you know. It's all happened before" . . . and then I suddenly felt nervous, without a notebook and not quite sure what to say. I suggested an interview—say, maybe in Montreal, when he felt better. He agreed, and I made my escape.

The next night, still in Toronto, Dylan looked better onstage, sporting a hat for the first time along with his by-now regulation black suit, twisting his left heel in time with "Just Like Tom Thumb's Blues," working with organist Garth Hudson through "Ballad of a Thin Man," and leaving the stage with a spread-armed curtsy. The Band seemed inspired, especially with a near-perfect reading of "I Shall Be Released" by Richard Manuel. As before, Dylan fluffed the second and third lines of "The Times They Are A-Changin'," but the audience waited and roared for the main lines. On "Like a Rolling Stone," the audience, in perfect unison, fast-clapped along with the song. This is the one song no one listens to, the Dylan anthem, the cause for celebration. The concert is marked down as the best since the second show in Philly.

And Toronto, for many of the Band, is home—or, at least, home enough so that the party after the show reminds one of Big Pink. In one room is a gathering of the next of kin, folks, stepfolks and friends. Full of etiquette—it *is* after midnight, after all—they are chatting and listening to *Planet Waves* on a cheap "compact" hi-fi borrowed from the hotel; "Tough Mama" is playing, and on the television (TV sets in touring rock stars' hotel rooms are *always* on, no matter what's happening in the room) is a movie starring Jimmy Stewart and some tough mama, a red fright-wigged woman wielding a shotgun, and as Dylan begins the final chorus, the woman blows up a houseboat, and Levon Helm and Rick Danko enter the room, listening to the music again, still loving it. Once again, Ronnie Hawkins and wife are part of the party; Gordon Lightfoot will drop in, too, and, out in the hallway, I run into Dylan again. I tell him I was thrilled, chilled again by his show; he mentions, again, how he'd had a flu shot and that's why the previous night wasn't so hot, and we affirm our plans to meet in Montreal.

The gathering is dissipating, and in another room, a drunken would-be groupie demands Dylan's presence. She staggers around, going nowhere slow, until Dylan shows up, asking for a blanket. She shouts at him, and Dylan goes into his I-don't-understand routine, slips into the bathroom and out again, before she notices. Later, Renee, a tall, blonde beauty, is talking with Robbie Robertson. Robbie, who looks years younger than he did in the Big Pink days, when his chin-thin beard, glasses and dark clothing gave him the look of a devout Russian Orthodox Jew, is listening attentively, like a priest. He seems to be humoring her, but no one can tell.

"I'm writing songs and I play guitar," she tells him.

Robbie, in a light fauntleroy hat, reddish-plaid shirt and bell-bottomed overalls, lets his sleepy eyes widen and his mouth open, as if the news may yet bowl him over.

"Really?" he says. "Gee, you and I do the same things. What a coincidence."

The woman has to leave. She has to go to work tomorrow morning. "But I don't want to be a secretary all my life," she tells Robbie. Robbie nods. He probably felt the same way 15 years ago, when he left school in Toronto to take up the guitar with the Robots.

I had met Robbie at the Nickelodeon; the next day, we met in his room and talked about the tour—how it started, exactly, how the Band felt being largely considered a backup, despite their co-billing and no matter how strong the applause at the end of each Band number and segment.

"We expected it," he said, "because we know who Bob is, right? And because we also knew that it had been eight years since he had ever done a tour, and we knew it was going to be an incredible level of anticipation for his music. We just can't . . . we have a job to do. You can't say to yourself, 'Oh, my god. Call Bob. Tell Bob he's got to get back out here.' The first time we played with him, when we walked out there, people would actually start booing and throwing things, so this is actually like a big, big departure. This is nothing, to have a couple of people yell, 'Dylan!' "

The Band and Dylan, said Robertson, have always thought about touring since the last tour, in 1966. "We were going to do another one, and Bob had the motorcycle wreck. And for a long time it didn't seem like a good idea to us at all. All of a sudden it started to become clear. There was a space, an opening, a necessity, almost, that just pulled you into it. It was no clever maneuver on anybody's behalf to put the thing together, to expand our audience or get a few extra albums. Everybody just felt the same way at the same time."

The impetus was a rock concert—the all-time biggest festival gathering, the 600,000-populated Watkins Glen festival.

"There was something different about it," he said. "At Watkins Glen we were playing, and we would do little things, intricate, subtle things that the audience would react to that I'd never seen them react to before. There was an alertness to the audience that I could not believe. And it was also, by far, the nicest of those festivals that we've played."

The whole thing is especially ironic because the Band is almost as reclusive as Dylan, having not played any dates for a year and a half before Watkins Glen, choosing to spend their time with families, working on albums, and playing with Dylan.

"We didn't want to play Watkins Glen at all. We were in a mood; we thought tours, those things . . . it's only the money, that's the only reason that you do it. But we were talked into it. You know the Grateful Dead, the Allman Brothers, really terrific people, and it was just one of those [Robbie puts on a painful, friendly, urging voice], 'Oh, come *on* . . . it's just up the road. You don't have to really go out of your way.' You know. 'Don't be a spoil sport.' That's what happened."

After the festival, an enthusiastic Robertson told Dylan about the new sensations he'd received. "And he went for it all the way. He asked me more questions. And then for a year or two I was planning on going to Malibu; I was ready to leave Woodstock. When I went out there we picked up on our talks and at this point it was more advanced, and we were coming out with a more positive attitude."

Now, on tour, did the Band and Dylan find confirmation for his feelings after Watkins Glen? "I don't think it's a similar situation," said Robbie. "I don't think it's necessarily the same audience. I also think that the audiences on this tour are not quite able to relax either. I think they're a little confused, a little nervous. I think they're waiting so much for something in there that it really distracts from that other thing that was in Watkins Glen."

But the Band and Dylan are nervous, too, said Robertson, and that partly explains the lack of communication from the artists to the audience, beyond the music and a wave, a peace sign or a clenched fist here, a nod from Robbie's guitar there. First, Robertson maintains, there's no need to talk. You say hello by showing up onstage; you play familiar music and don't need to introduce numbers. A new number from Dylan is obviously new. "So you're kind of . . . its meaningless talk."

"Just remember, when Bob first started to play, he used to do more talking than music. He used to just talk and talk and tell stories, jokes and carrying on, you know. It's a different thing. And also, I think in his case, everybody takes it to such a degree that it's embarrassing, almost, to say anything. I mean, they start, you know . . ."

To analyze what he meant by "We'll be back in 15 minutes"?

"Right, they start counting to fifteen backwards . . . they just take it and they get silly."

One critic in Chicago, a man with a background in theater, accused Dylan of holding back and concluded: "Maybe Dylan just isn't a performer."

Dylan, in Montreal, responded: "They just don't understand." He shrugged his shoulders. "It's got nothing to do with that kind of atmosphere. What the critics expect is what they expect. It concerns me more with getting it to the people.

"It's basically music, not a music-hall routine."

Another reason for the silence between numbers, said Robertson, is the group's required concentration on the music at hand. A song changes from one night to another, said Robertson, and Dylan loves to pull surprises.

"He pulled one out of the hat last night, that we had never played, or ran over, or even considered: 'It Takes a Lot to Laugh.' "

The Band and Dylan went through some 80 numbers in one four-hour session, said Robertson, so that the show can change every night. But rehearsals, he said, were impossible. "For our situation and our mentality, it seemed so absurd to get into a room and run over 'Positively Fourth Street.' We'd go, 'What is this? Remember the kickoff? Who cares what the kickoff was?' You know. We just can't approach it like that."

Rehearsals began three months before the tour. "We sat down and played for four hours and ran over an incredible number of tunes. Just instantly. We would request tunes. Bob would ask us to play certain tunes of ours, and then we would do the same, then we'd think of some that we would particularly like to do. And then it was over, we said, 'That's it.' "

So, onstage, oftentimes a song will end quite abruptly; another may wheeze and fizzle to a tardy conclusion; Dylan will stop a number to change the beat.

Even while planning the tour, Dylan and the Band were nervous, said Robertson. "Not a real emotional nervousness, but also a physical endurance nervousness. Like Bob was saying, 'Shit, I haven't done nothing in eight years, all of a sudden I'm going to go out there and hit it for 40 concerts?' We're not really outgoing people," Robbie said again, "we're just not the kind of people that can—'Sure, turn us loose!' "

Once the tour was certain, the Band would call Bill Graham, whom they had worked with, doing concerts, and David Geffen, chairman of Elektra/Asylum Records, now Dylan's label.

When asked about how he got to know Robbie, Geffen replied: "He's just my friend." Robbie's version had less of the hangout aura to it: "He called me up once, about nine or ten months ago. Just out of the blue, he said he wanted to see me. I talked to him and found him interesting. I thought he was in tune with today, now. He wasn't relying on what it was, or he didn't have ridiculous theories on what it should be or will be." What triggered the call? Was it just to get to know you?

"No, it was a business move."

Robertson told Dylan about Graham and Geffen, Dylan approved, and the two went to work, convincing the group that if they were to avoid box-office riots, they had to play more than ten dates, and in larger-than-theater halls. It was also Graham who proposed the ticket prices (criticized in some cities as too high, averaging $8 and reaching a top of $9.50), and the Band and Dylan—who left all money matters to their various attorneys and to Geffen and Graham—agreed.

"The decision," said Robbie, "was made by Bill and David, and they put their logic together and explained it to us. We left it up to them because they could be a little bit more objective than us. They would say, 'Listen, Joe Blow gets $7.50. Just Joe Blow, so I would think you guys should charge that, and if there's two of you, then you should charge' . . . and they had all kinds of reasons. 'If you don't, then people are going to think that something is wrong.' Me? I just said, 'You know better than we do.' You have to give people room to move around in and do things. If you do it all yourself you go crazy."

And when the Band and Dylan were informed that the tour would gross $5 million and net at least half that, no one felt that it was a bit much? Or asked if it was really needed or deserved?

"No way do we feel we deserve it," Robertson replied calmly. "I think the whole thing is so out of proportion it doesn't make any sense at all. But I don't think a gallon of gas is worth a dollar, either. I think that the whole thing is so out of proportion, you couldn't just step in and say, 'Wait a minute, everybody.' That's not our job. You can't go around deciding for the world what the price for everything should be. We could have charged $2. That could have been a good move or a bad move. Who knows?"

Dylan echoed Robbie: "I put it in Bill Graham's

hands," he said. "I just let people know I was ready." He added: "Originally, I wanted to play small halls, but I was just talked out of that."

Graham himself said that he could have suggested a high of $20, and still sell out the tour, just to prove the point "that the market will bear it. But that's not what I was trying to prove. I tried to make it a decent price that I didn't think there'd be complaints on."

Each show in the first four cities was sold out; but in Chicago and Philadelphia, concerts were not sold out until nearly the last minute. In Chicago, last-minute shuffling of sound and lighting equipment made 1000 seats available for two shows, and they were sold on the days of the shows. In Philadelphia, at the time of the first show, at 2 PM, there were still tickets for the third show, the next night, available at the box office.

Graham maintained that it *was* an immediate sellout, dating back to the December 2nd placement of ads in every city on the tour. Thousands of ticket requests had been returned then, he said. But 99% of requests had been for the night shows, leaving day-show tickets unsold. Also, he said, just two weeks before (that would be around Christmas), it was discovered that some side seats, with "obstructed views," could be sold, and ads were placed announcing "obstructed" tickets for $8. But, according to a Spectrum employee, the 19,000-seat auditorium sold some 16,000 seats for each show in the first rush, and placed ads on WMMR-FM by December 8th.

Later, we learned that Madison Square Garden, on January 17th, announced more tickets available for the New York shows. Graham and Geffen had previously reported an estimated 1.2 million ticket requests in the New York area; now, for some last-minute reason, the Garden, which can hold 58,500 people for three shows, had seats to spare.

Every show ends up sold out, of course. And in Philadelphia, the only city outside New York to have Dylan and the Band for more than two shows, writer Jon Takiff remarked: "It's pretty phenomenal to sell out three shows at the Spectrum."

Still, the facts seemed to make so much hype-confetti of Graham and Geffen's pre-tour claims of a nationwide, overnight, mail-order sellout.

Bill Graham, the man who has an answer for just about anything, was even equipped with the proper languages for this tour. In Montreal, at the end of the first concert at the Forum, after the encore, he told the crowd, in fluid French, that Dylan had gone and would not be back. The next night, the voice that has sent countless antagonists up against countless walls was again soothing and Frenchy, telling the people to please not smoke and crowd into the center aisle. Both Montreal audiences would proceed to smoke, the smell coming out like a mixture of rubber and Baco-Bits; they would crowd into the aisles—because, said Graham, fearful auditorium guards refused to try and block the aisles by themselves; and they would drink, sneaking in bottles of Rouge Sec wine, a product of Quebec.

The Forum is used by all the big rock acts, a student from Quebec City told me. Jethro Tull, Ten Years After, the Moody Blues. What about, er, French groups? "They play the small place—the Sports Centre at the University of Montreal."

It is a bilingual crowd, you can tell by the chatter around you. But, the student said, "I read there are 6000 Americans here tonight." Because of the language situation, said Graham, Montreal was the only city to sell tickets through box offices, and thousands of people had crossed the border to get tickets and, a month later, to attend the show.

One woman, who came to Montreal from Plattsburgh, New York, seemed disappointed with Dylan, after "Lay Lady Lay." It was the new way he had of singing it, no longer country-comfy and inviting, but snarl-joking, stretching last words and snapping them off with a grit of his teeth.

"I liked the old Dylan," said the woman, an employee at the state college in Plattsburgh. "Here, on this song, I felt he was ripping me off, just singing a song to get through it. He's not sharing a part of himself with us." She broke into applause, minutes later, when Dylan went into "The Times They Are A-Changin'," and joined the ovation while Dylan offered two bows and a clenched left fist. She nodded her approval again as the solo Dylan worked his way through "Gates of Eden." And when "Rolling Stone" came around, she was on top of her chair, standing atop her cotton coat and clapping along. (Dylan: " 'Like a Rolling Stone' is just as real today as it was then. The audience is reacting the same as back then. It was always the one that got the best reaction.") And here, when Dylan returned for the encore, the ovation continued on, and did not die, the way it had in the other cities.

"Always love to come back to Montreal."

While friends of Dylan said he had stayed off the road mostly because his family came first, he left his wife and children behind. With him on the first few stops of the tour was Louie Kemp, a friend of Bob's since the days in Hibbing when they went to camp together. Louie stuck close to Dylan, from hotel to hotel, and accompanied him wherever he went. In Chicago, they checked out a show at the Earl of Old Town. In Philadelphia, Dylan spent off-hours ice-skating. In Toronto, he planned to see *The Exorcist* at a local university movie house, then canceled out. He visited with a friend, a talent agent named Roberta Richards, and they talked about an artist Ms. Richards had handled: Leon Redbone. Later, she would bring John Donebie backstage at the Maple Leaf Gardens, and Donebie would have the usual: He thanked Dylan for 12 years of music, and Dylan told him, "It's all right."

In Montreal, Dylan also took it easy, staying on a diet of vegetables, fruits, herb tea and distilled water. His one known foray into the streets—aside from shopping trips—was to pick up a loose NO PARKING sign to take back home. I remember a Rodney Bingenheimer story about him and Dylan driving around Hollywood one night in search of signs; now, propped up against a couch in his suite, there was the evidence of such a hobby.

On the scheduled day of the interview, I waited through

the morning and early afternoon. When Dylan's supposed to call, you don't go running down to the newsstand to leaf through pube magazines. I decided to busy myself by going over my notes from the seven shows I'd seen and compiling a list that would tell me, in case I ever got interested, just which songs Dylan was doing most often, and how many different numbers he had done in his concerts so far, at an average of 18 songs per night, with the Band adding another nine or ten.

It turned out that Dylan indeed had—and played—favorites. Of 32 songs he had tried thus far, 12 numbers had appeared in, at least, six of seven concerts. In every show, he had performed "Lay Lady Lay," "Ballad of a Thin Man," "All Along the Watchtower," "It's Alright, Ma." "Like a Rolling Stone," and two from *Planet Waves,* "Forever Young" and "Something There Is About You."

"Just Like Tom Thumb's Blues," "It Ain't Me Babe," "Knockin' on Heaven's Door," and a new number, "Except You," had been done in every show but one, and "Most Likely You Go Your Way (And I'll Go Mine)" had been sung seven times in five concerts.

"I Don't Believe You" had been done five times, scattered out evenly, and "Ballad of Hollis Brown" was also a five-timer. "Times They Are A-Changin' " had been done twice in Chicago, and once each in Toronto and Montreal. (Having stumbled through lines each time he tried the song, Dylan got a present from Bill Graham at intermission of the second show in Montreal: a set of cue cards, the lyrics to this, one of his best-known—if not by him—compositions written out in two-inch-high letters. Dylan laughed, then marched out and substituted "Blowin' in the Wind" in the "Times" slot.

The rest of the list included one-time acoustic shots of "To Ramona," "Mama, You've Been on My Mind," "Song to Woody," "Maggie's Farm," "As I Went Out One Morning," and "It Takes a Lot to Laugh (It Takes a Train to Cry)." Twice each, he had done "Rainy Day Women (Nos. 12 & 35)," "Just Like a Woman," "Hero Blues," "Love Minus Zero (No Limit)," "Gates of Eden," "Girl From the North Country," "Don't Think

Twice, It's All Right," and the new "Wedding Song." Three times each, he had performed "Tough Mama" (another new, gritty love song), "Leopard Skin Pillbox Hat," and one of his own stated favorites from the protest days, "The Lonesome Death of Hattie Carroll."

"It's more interesting for me to be able to move things around," said Dylan. "These are the songs that were important for us, for me, for people we knew. They're mostly songs that've been recorded through the years."

I hadn't heard any songs from *New Morning* or *Self-Portrait* yet, I said.

"Well, we'll do some from *New Morning.* We've got three or four numbers. But *Self-Portrait,* I didn't live with those songs for too long. Those were just scraped together." To, say, pay some sort of tribute to the songwriters you liked? Dylan smiled and nodded.

Dylan and I exchanged admissions of nervousness; soon enough, we were comfortable. He's been well-known to be antagonistic during interviews, challenging the wording of questions, offering totally evasive or fabricated responses. He does, in fact, give mostly half-answers, and one is not encouraged to pursue his replies. His face says to take a second to let it soak in, see the self-evidence for yourself. If he was putting me on with any of his responses—say, in his promotion man's dream of an answer about doing his old songs—then he was a good actor. And, as he said during our hour session, he's not a movie star.

The first time we'd talked, Dylan had mentioned a special enthusiasm for doing the Texas dates, in Fort Worth and in Houston January 25th and 26th, just before the five New York shows.

"Maybe it's just the Mexican influence," he said. "They're more receptive to my kind of music, my kind of style," said Dylan. "In the old days . . ." he paused. "I hate to call them the 'old days,' " he thought out loud, and laughed. "Anyway, I did New York, San Francisco and Austin. The rest were hard in coming."

The tour, he said, wasn't planned to take advantage of a lull in the music business, or to make a statement in a time of national crisis. "I saw daylight," he said. "I just took off."

Did he miss being onstage?

"Sure," he replied. "There's always those butterflies at a certain point, but then there's the realization that the songs I'm singing mean as much to the people as to me; so it's just up to me to perform the best I can."

What kind of feeling did he get, singing the "protest" and "message" songs again, especially considering what people might read in his decision to revive those songs?

"For me, it's just reinforcing those images in my head that were there, that don't die, that will be there tomorrow. And in doing so for myself, hopefully also for those people who also had those images."

In an earlier chat, Dylan had implied that it was a "new time," in which people were united in their political thinking. I mentioned a comment by a member of the Committee, that much of the country still needed turning around, as evidenced by the overwhelming reelection of Richard Nixon, after four years of fairly obvious nonsense, and by the underwhelming call, at this point, for his removal.

"Sure," Dylan agreed, "there's still a message. But the same electric spark that went off back then could still go off again—the spark that led to nothing. Our kids will probably protest, too. Protest is an old thing. Sometimes protest is deeper, or different—the Haymarket Riot, the Russian Revolution, the Civil War—that's protest.

"There's always a need for protest songs. You just gotta tap it."

What, I asked Dylan, had he been doing to keep his vocal cords in shape? Had he been singing regularly, at home, through the years off the stage? He said he hadn't. "We've been through the big tours before," he said. "Actually, I'd like to have a little club where I could sing when I felt like it."

What about the changes his voice and vocal style have gone through over the past few albums? Dylan looked past me, then out the window again. "That's a good question. I don't know. I could only guess—if it *has* changed. I've never gone for having a great voice, for cultivating one. I'm still not doing it now."

As for the rearrangements of songs, the harder, snappier way he's singing some of the older songs: "You'll always stretch things out or cut it up, just to keep interested. If you can't stay interested that way, you'll have to lose track. But I'm me now, that's the way it comes out."

What? You're meaner now?

"What? Oh, no. I'm *me* now." Dylan laughed. He could just see the headline.

Is Dylan planning to stay in Malibu?

"No," he said, "we're just there temporarily. It was cold in New York and we didn't want to go back there after Mexico [and the shooting of *Pat Garrett and Billy the Kid*]. I can't stay away from New York!"

How did he get the role of Alias in the Sam Peckinpah film?

"Just one thing into another. [Pause] They took me on because I was a big name. I've seen myself on screen; movies don't impress me. That part didn't scare me off at all. I just hoped I didn't get shot during the movie.

"I don't know who I played. I tried to play whoever it was in the story, but I guess it's a known fact in history that there was nobody who was the character I played in the story.

"No, I don't want to be a movie star," he continued, "but I've got a vision to put up on the screen. Someday we'll get around to doing it. The Peckinpah experience was valuable, in terms of getting near the big action."

Would Dylan do more films before tackling his "vision"?

"The Peckinpah movie brought me as close as I'll get," he said. "I've been on sets of movies and TV shows, but they were small-time compared. They spent $4.5 million on *Billy the Kid,* had all the top people. So that was really heavy, gave me that vibration. When I finally do mine, it'll have that vibration."

What about his latest business moves?

"I don't think about it," said Dylan. "Just had to get

out of some legal hassles from back in the old days."

Dylan, in earlier announcements, had planned to have his own label, ironically named Ashes & Sand, the name of the holding company he'd set up back in the old, Albert Grossman days. Dylan smiled, laughing at himself:

"That only lasted a quick few minutes," he agreed.

What were the advantages to having his own label? Was Dylan advised by an outside party to form his own company? "I advised myself it was a good thing, and then I advised myself that it wasn't. I just didn't need it."

Dylan does, however, maintain an interest in spotting —and helping—new talent. If Ashes & Sand were a reality, Dylan said, he'd want Leon Redbone.

"Leon interests me," he said. "I've heard he's anywhere from 25 to 60. I've been this close"—Dylan held his hands out, a foot and a half apart—"and I can't tell. But you gotta see him. He does old Jimmie Rodgers, then turns around and does a Robert Johnson." Redbone has surfaced at various folk festivals in the past few years and is every bit the mystery that Dylan indicates.

And what about the other Leon, Leon Russell, who produced only a couple of cuts with Dylan?

"Leon and I, we didn't do that much." Dylan couldn't remember exactly what they'd done, beyond "Watching the River Flow" and "When I Paint My Masterpiece."

"It went fine, it was as good as it could've been expected to be. But the producers that have meant the most to me are Tom Wilson, John Hammond and Bob Johnston. They were there. They were there when . . . well, it's like a small group of friends."

What about the *Dylan* album, the collection of *Self-Portrait* outtakes Columbia had released on the eve of the Dylan tour, after Dylan split from the label to go with Ashes & Sand, and then Asylum? Dave Geffen had charged Columbia with holding the album over Dylan's head, threatening to release it unless he re-signed his contract. "That's when they sealed their doom," Geffen said. Speaking on Dylan's behalf earlier in the tour, Geffen had characterized Dylan's response to the album as utter repudiation. "He disclaims it," Geffen said. "He doesn't know that Dylan."

(Columbia's vice president of A&R, Charles Koppelman, denied Geffen's allegations. The album was delayed, at Dylan's request, during contract talks, he said, but Dylan had never expressed disapproval with the album itself. "He called Goddard [Lieberson, president of Columbia] and said he didn't mind us at all putting out the album," Koppelman said. The executive couldn't offer much explanation for the sloppiness of the album: the lack of information on dates of recording, backup musicians and even composers' credits. "We had a lack of information ourselves," he said. Columbia, Koppelman said, will continue to release Dylan material. "We have a fairly good amount of tape," including live concerts and "a group of tapes where he performed with other well-known performers. We have a good few albums," said Koppelman.)

Dylan described the material on *Dylan* as outtakes, sung "just to warm up," he said. "They were just not to be used. I thought it was well understood." But, he said, he couldn't understand all the critical downgrading of the album.

"I didn't think it was that bad, really!" he said.

Dylan said he thought Clive Davis, the president of Columbia Records, fired last May for alleged "financial malfeasance," was "a scapegoat." But even if Davis was still at Columbia, he said, he would've left the label. "It was long overdue," he said. "Just a gut feeling it was time to go on. I suspected they were doing more talk than action. Just released 'em and that's all. I got a feeling they didn't care whether I stayed there or not."

As for David Geffen: "He's there." What does "there" mean?

"Whatever it takes to be there."

Has he signed a contract with Asylum, as Geffen said?

"I'm not so sure we signed one. I don't sign anything these days."

It's been a tour of luck and coincidences, running into Neil Young's father, Ronnie Hawkins and Bob Dylan himself. But there was also the leaflet I picked up outside the Nickelodeon, blood-red headlined: 40 DAYS! AND NINEVEH SHALL BE DESTROYED. It was dated November 12th and distributed by the Children of God, a local religion franchise. "Forty Days," of course, was Ronnie Hawkins' first major hit.

Here, sitting with Dylan, I also thought about the headlines that had surfaced upon his arrival in Philadelphia and Toronto. In Philly, the *Evening Bulletin* carried a story: "Fewer Jews Reported in Philadelphia Area" (population decreased 7% in the last year). In Toronto, Dylan was greeted with this headline in the *Globe and Mail:* "Apathy, Alienation Reported Rampant Among Young Jews."

"It is not the slightest bit surprising (but nonetheless shocking and depressing) that no less than 88% [of converts to Christianity] consider the Jewish religion 'valueless,'" said the report issued by P'eylim of Canada, a Toronto Jewish organization.

Religious images have long been part of Bob Dylan's music. In 1971, he visited the Wailing Wall in Israel. Now, on tour, it was rumored that he was planning on handing over his cut of the profits to the Israeli cause; that he was an "ultra-Zionist."

"I'm not sure what a Zionist really is," he said, putting down the rumors as "just gossip." As for the religious images that surface regularly in his music, he commented, after a good pause: "Religion to me is a fleeting thing. Can't nail it down. It's in me and out of me. It does give me, on the surface, some images, but I don't know to what degree.

"Like da Vinci going in to paint the *Last Supper*. Until he finishes it, no one knows what the *Last Supper* is. He goes out and finds 12 guys, puts them around this table, and there's your *Last Supper*. Or Moses. He found a guy and painted him, and, forever, that guy will be Moses. But why Moses or the *Last Supper?* Why not a flower? Or a tree?"

Dylan had earlier mentioned an astrological influence on his return to active performance, the removal of an obstacle, Saturn, in his planetary system. I asked him to elaborate.

"I can't read anybody's chart," he said, "but the thing about Saturn is, I didn't know what it was at the time, or I would've gone somewhere away. It's a big, heavy obstacle that comes into your chain of events that fucks you up in a big way. It came into my chart a few years ago and just flew off again a couple of months ago."

Who'd clued him in on Saturn?

"Someone very dear to me."

The Band with Dylan: "It's Right on the Dot"

By Ben Fong-Torres

See the man with the stage fright
Just standing up there to give it all his might
And he got caught in the spotlight
But when you get to the end, you want to start all
over again*

The Toronto crowd whooped in approval. After all, Dylan had just finished his sixth number, "The Ballad of a Thin Man," had offered a quick bow, had moved down the stage steps and into his modest backstage quarters, leaving the Band on its own. Now Rick Danko marched up to the mike, past the booming guitar intro:

Now deep in the heart of the lonely kid
Who suffered so much for what he did
They gave this ploughboy his fortune and fame
Since that day he ain't been the same*

* "Stage Fright," copyright, ©, 1970, by Jaime R. Robertson.

"It's accidental," said Robbie Robertson, the Band's lead guitarist, spokesman, and composer of "Stage Fright."

"I mean, it was not put there because [he whistled a brain-stormed, what-a-clever-idea whistle] 'If we do this *here! . . .'* at all. The key that 'Stage Fright' is in, coming after the song before it—it's a nice lift. It's picked musically and for its tempo. It's not necessarily picked because it's relevant to this or that."

"Stage Fright" is, in fact, "about ourselves," said Robertson. "We're those kind of people—not outgoing, basically shy. We've never been very comfortable showing off. We play music, write songs and like to play them, but we have never and will never really have it in the palm of our hand. And we don't want to. We enjoy that rush of being scared. A lot of people I've gone to see, it just seems to roll off their tongue. They don't seem to sweat. You see no pain in them whatsoever. It's just a wonderful evening of entertainment. It's not for us. It's turmoil. It's pulled out like a tooth."

But the music is at least as painstaking as it is painful. Doing ten songs of their own each concert and backing up Dylan on another thirteen each show, the Band is winning over each audience it faces. And that is not an easy achievement, given the complete absorption by each audience in the anticipated presence, the overriding mystique, of Dylan.

One critic of the Band complained about their "blasé professionalism." Others hear it as a precise execution of some of the best, most thoughtful and picturesque American rock & roll ever, mostly by Jaime "Robbie" Robertson. And the Band (Robertson on lead guitar, Levon Helm on drums and vocals, Rick Danko on bass and vocals, Richard Manuel on keyboards and vocals, and Garth Hudson on organ) is not and cannot be a machine, as it has to roll with Dylan's musical changes of mind almost every show.

We are at the Inn on the Park in Toronto. On the way here to this hotel in Don Valley, we passed through a part of town, hidden by snow in the night, that got Robbie smiling: "This is Cabbagetown," he said. "You know, on the cover of *Moondog Matinee?* I described the feeling of the place to the artist, and he got it just perfect." Robèrtson and all of the Band, except Levon, are from Canada, and he's quite at ease, talking with a low voice, at a slow gait.

The touring history of the Band, since their emergence in 1968 from the big pink house in Woodstock, is a simple one: They've done as little as possible, taking a year and a half off between the recorded concert in New York, December 31, 1971, and a Watkins Glen appearance in July, 1973. Then nothing until the Dylan tour. The Band prefer to stay home with families—all are now in Malibu, along with the Bob Dylan family—and work on albums.

And, as Robertson repeated several times, in various contexts, the Band are not "very in-touch people," and they don't relate to much of the current rock scene. There is more than a touch of elitism when Robertson states: "We don't have fancy outfits or sparklers on our eyes, and we don't cut off our heads."

But even the albums come hard. After *Rock Of Ages,* the live set from New Year's Eve at the Academy of Music, Robertson considered a few soundtrack offers, then decided to do another album of original songs. He'd written a few tunes, he said, and the Band began the album; then he shifted into another gear. He had been listening to the avant-garde classical music of Krzysztof Penderecki.

"I bought one of his albums a few years ago because I liked the album cover: It was a guy holding a candle. Very spooky-looking cover. One day I put it on and I thought, 'My God. That's terrific.' I think he is the contemporary classical writer of this age.

"He doesn't just use strings or orchestras. He uses very unorthodox techniques. He uses guitars and 30 men singing at half an octave below their range. It's incredible, what he reaches for, and I like very much the lyrics that he writes and I find his music haunting. Other people's music I can shake off very easily. His music I cannot sluff off like that."

Robertson's own writing, however, is not outwardly changed by his admiration for Penderecki. "Just like you could be influenced by Leadbelly; it doesn't mean that you'll write Leadbelly tunes. It just means you like him, but you don't necessarily do anything similar to what he does at all. But Penderecki is who I've listened to to get where I am now, musically."

So Robertson and the Band began putting together a new, more ambitious album. "More of a works than just some songs," he said. "But after getting into it for a while I realized that it was much more involved and advanced, that it took a whole other kind of writing and attention. You couldn't knock them off the way you could other things. So after about halfway into it we said we got to do something. I mean we got to do something to just say hello to everybody again. We were fooling around one day and we played a couple of tunes that we used to play years ago, and it was really fun, and we said, 'Gee, why don't we do our old nightclub act?'

"It seemed like people wouldn't object to that at this point because a lot of people feel nostalgic, because what's happening now is kind of watery and they're picking the past apart again, so it seemed to make sense.

"It wasn't as easy as I thought. A lot of the tunes were hard to get into seriously. I mean, to do 'Bony Maronie'—you listen to it and you say, 'Whew!' It was fine, but we don't mean it. We *can't* mean 'Bony Maronie.' So the ones we picked are the ones we believed the most."

The result was *Moondog Matinee* (named after Alan Freed's Cleveland radio show of 1951, *The Moon Dog Show* on WJW), featuring tunes like "The Great Pretender," "I'm Ready," "Mystery Train," "Holy Cow," and "Share Your Love."

Next would be the album with Dylan, cut in three days in November at Village Recorders studio in Los Angeles. Robertson, who supervised the sound on the album and mixed it, with Village chief engineer Rob Fraboni, was enthusiastic: "Oh, man, what a record! And it just gets better and better and better. The more you live with it. It happened so quick and it's great. It's just right on the dot."

Why did it happen so quick?

"We were not going to play around," said Robertson. "Drive it into the ground."

Fraboni, 23, previously worked with Dylan in 1971—at the Record Plant in New York on the Allen Ginsberg album with Dylan as back-up. It was never released, said Fraboni, because "it wasn't on the commercial side."

Robbie had heard about the studio, which included a new room and monitoring system put together by Fraboni. "He heard it was tight," the engineer said. "And it's out of town (in West L.A., near Westwood). When the Stones were there it was comfortable for them; they had security." (Dylan and the Band were booked under the names "Judge Magney," a name picked by studio general manager Dick La Palm and, coincidentally, a rest stop on Highway 61 along the Minnesota border). The only visitors to the sessions were Cher Bono (friend of Elektra/Asylum head David Geffen), Geffen himself and Jackie DeShannon and Donna Weiss, who sang backup on one track. "It was good," Fraboni said, "but it had a different feel and wasn't left in."

Only three songs required overdubs, Fraboni recalled: "Going Going Gone," "Never Say Goodbye," and "On a Night Like This."

Two of the songs, Fraboni said, were worked out completely in the studio: "Dirge" and "Wedding Song."

"One Saturday afternoon, after the cutting with the Band was finished, we were putting together a master reel. Dylan was writing 'Wedding Song.' He told me he wanted to record. So I set up some mikes and we let it roll, and that was the take. You'll hear some noises on the track; those are from buttons on his sleeve hitting the guitar."

Next for the Band, according to Robertson, will be either a live album from Watkins Glen, the "works" album, or another record with Dylan.

Finally, the Band is yet to decide its business future. David Geffen, the man who brought Dylan into the Elektra/Asylum, had told me he's also signed the Band. Robertson denied it. What about after their commitment to Capitol, consisting of two more albums?

"Hmmm . . . I'm not sure," he said. "I think we have our hands full with other things. I'm not thinking about that too much, really. It's not very interesting to think about. And it will just kind of take care of itself in the next few months."

Dylan in Atlanta: "Great to Be in Joe-jah!"

By Paul West

In this, the ninth city of his 21-city tour with the Band, Bob Dylan opened himself up to some peach-sweet Southern hospitality, as he socialized with Jimmy Carter, the governor of Georgia, at a post-concert party at the governor's mansion.

Carter, a Democrat who entertains 1976 vice-presidential hopes, sent Dylan a hand-written invitation last December, promising that any gathering would not be open to the press. "It was not an effusive note," Carter said later. Dylan accepted, through tour-producer Bill Graham, with a special request for some real down-home cuisine.

Following the first concert of a two-day stopover in Atlanta, January 21st and 22nd, Dylan and his entourage rolled up to the mansion on Atlanta's posh northwest side in three long black limousines escorted by a state trooper and entered the boxlike, tin-roofed neo-Georgian residence which stands as a monument to its first occupant, former-Governor Lester Maddox.

Inside, the group was met by Carter, a 49-year-old peanut farmer and former nuclear submarine captain, his wife, Rosalynn, and their three sons, one of whom, Chip, made a pilgrimage to Woodstock in December, 1968, just to shake Dylan's hand. The party in Atlanta was Chip's idea, the kind of fantasy that apparently can come true if you happen to be the governor's son.

For more than two hours, 30 persons, including Dylan, the Band, promoter Bill Graham, three heavies from Georgia's fledgling music industry in Macon—Alex Hodges, head of Paragon Agency, which manages the Allman Brothers, Phil Walden and Frank Fenner of Capricorn Records—and the Carter sons' closest friends, ate grits, scrambled eggs and country ham, drank beer and wine and dipped fresh vegetables in a cheese sauce.

The governor acted as Dylan's personal host, guiding him through the mansion, pointing out antiques and chatting quietly.

"I asked him if he wanted a drink, but he only wanted orange juice and would only eat the vegetables," Carter reported the next morning.

At one point Dylan and the governor slipped outside for a private walk around the mansion grounds. They talked about the tour, Dylan's plans to return home afterwards, his family, and the responsibility Dylan feels toward his audience.

Asked if Dylan had discussed the persistent rumors that he plans to donate his share of the tour royalties to Israel, Carter replied, "He didn't say anything to me about it."

Earlier, however, during intermission at the concert, Graham met the governor at Carter's sixth-row seat (officials of the hall had given the governor's party 16 seats on the row, but the Carters had insisted on paying for them) and told the governor: "Dylan was particularly impressed by the fact that you had gone to Israel." Carter, a strong Israel supporter, toured the Holy Land in 1972.

At the party, however, Carter said, "When I mentioned Israel, Dylan changed the subject and said he and his wife had recently been to Mexico and had enjoyed that country, too." (The next day, Chip Carter brought Dylan a gift from his father, a small coin found at an Israeli archeological dig.)

Others at the party, including Carter, reported Dylan's famous reticence: "He never initiates conversation, but he'll answer a question if you ask him." Carter, who seemed sincerely interested in both the Dylan phenomenon and the man himself, called Dylan "painfully timid" but found a warm, family-loving man behind the electric stage personality and the reclusive private self.

By 1:30 AM the party ended and Dylan returned to his hotel room. Shortly afterward, Gregg Allman and his wife appeared at the door of the governor's mansion and Carter came downstairs in blue jeans and bare feet ("the way I always dress around the house") to say hello and tell them how sorry he was they had missed the party.

(In Miami, where the two Dylan concerts on January 19th caused a nine-mile-long traffic jam that kept many people from entering the Sportatorium until the concert was half over, there were only two protest signs and six demonstrators. The signs read: "$9.50—A RIP OFF" and "DYLAN: MASTER OF WAR," referring to the Dylan-as-Zionist rumors.

(Away from the concerts, Dylan, who stayed in a hotel in nearby Coconut Grove, ventured out to the folk and blues club, Bubba's, and, on Sunday, joined the end of a religious rally at Peacock Park. The rally was conducted by Arthur Blessitt, once known as "The Mod Minister of Sunset Strip," and, according to a reporter at the Miami Herald, "Bob went up and talked to Blessitt for about ten minutes. My feeling was that he was just inquiring. Art didn't want to say anything about it. He said 'If anybody is going to talk about it, it'll have to be Bob Dylan.' "

(In Washington, Dylan wasn't in a mood to talk to any reporters, after reading a *Washington Post* article by Tom Zito, who had interviewed Dylan in Boston, early on the morning of January 15th. Zito asked Dylan about the Bangladesh concert and why Dylan didn't do any political benefits. "There were millions of people starving in Bangladesh," Dylan replied. "George McGovern wasn't starving. He just wanted to be President." He continued: "Actually, maybe the problem is that I don't like the Democratic-Republican system. I like monarchies, kings, and queens."

(After the interview, Zito said, Dylan approached him in the hotel hallway: "Gee, do you think you could scratch that stuff about McGovern? It wasn't right for me to say it." Zito proceeded to include the McGovern quote and reported Dylan asking him to cut the material.

("That wasn't the agreement we made before the interview," Zito said, "that he'd have approval of what I wrote." Questioned further, Zito said there was no "agreement" of any sort made before the talk, but that "I felt I had to use it. I felt it was one of the few questions where he said something more than one sentence, something that came from inside him.")

In Atlanta, as pro-Arab demonstrators silently handed out literature to latecomers outside the concert hall, a relaxed Bob Dylan and his road manager played Ping-Pong backstage before facing 17,000 fans in the Omni, a new multi-use sports facility.

Dylan opened and encored both Atlanta concerts with a driving version of "Most Likely You'll Go Your Way (I'll Go Mine)," which could be the theme song of the tour. Following his second number, "Lay Lady Lay," Dylan said, "It's great to be back in *Joe*-jah," and finished the opening segment with "Just Like Tom Thumb's Blues," "Leopard-Skin Pillbox Hat," "It Ain't Me Babe," and (with Dylan on piano) "Subterranean Homesick Blues."

He closed the concerts with "Forever Young" and "Like a Rolling Stone." As the house lights went up during "Like a Rolling Stone," the crowd, which had been kept under extremely tight control all evening, began flowing toward the stage. With each "How does it feel?" the powerful spots, normally used to light sporting events, were turned on, creating new waves of energy. A fight suddenly broke out next to the governor's seat and police hauled away an excited young man.

Almost unnoticed in the frenzy of thousands standing and shouting from their seats, a young man pushed his bearded friend in a wheel chair toward the stage, highlighting the quasi-revivalist spirit of the evening, as Dylan encored with a reprise of "Most Likely You'll Go Your Way (I'll Go Mine)."

The following night, Dylan substituted "Rainy Day Women (Nos. 12 & 35)" for "Leopard-Skin Pillbox Hat," bringing gasps and cheers for his harp solos. And, in his solo spot, he played "It's All Over Now, Baby Blue" for the first time on the tour instead of "Just Like A Woman."

On the encore, the lines, "Time will tell who has fell, and who's been left behind," echoed with new meaning, for the Atlanta stop had raised new questions about the politics of the tour and the Dylan mystique.

Bob Dylan's Star-Studded Homecoming

By Loraine Alterman and Ben Fong-Torres

In Philadelphia, he'd told the audience, "It's great to be back in *Philly!*" In Montreal, he'd said: "It's great to be back in Montreal!" In Atlanta, he'd said: "It's great to be back in *Joe*-jah!" Three years ago, at the Isle of Wight, he'd told the British: "It's great to be here, sure is, sure is."

So it's always great. Bob Dylan loves it everywhere, even if he did tell *The New York Times,* in one of his five rare interviews, that being on tour was "like going from nowhere to nowhere."

But in New York, at Madison Square Garden on Thursday night, January 30th, when he said—you guessed it—"It's great to be back in New York," and added: "You're a great New York audience," there had to be much more going on inside Dylan's head. It had to be more than a perfunctory comment. And at the end of the matinee show that Thursday, he'd even added a promise that no one around him could confirm that "we'll see you next year." He said that to a crowd that had rung the Garden with a five-minute ovation and refused to leave, even after a second encore, "Blowin' in the Wind."

In other cities, Dylan would have loped down the wooden stage stairs, out through the backstage area and squeezed into a limousine or the tour's camper van by the time the audience had been applauding for a minute. This time, tour producer Bill Graham brought him back. Already changed from his black belted-back jacket into a blue and white Toronto hockey jersey, he took a final bow and made his promise.

(David Geffen, head of Asylum Records, on which Dylan's *Planet Waves* album was released, interpreted Dylan's statement as "a warm gesture to his audience." There are no plans as yet for a US tour next year, although a European tour has been discussed and remains a possibility.)

The matinee was possibly the high point of Dylan's New York dates—he performed twice at the Nassau Coliseum on Long Island and three times at Madison Square Garden—and New York itself had to be the high point of the entire 21-city tour.

Anthony Scaduto, 41, author of the most intimate biography yet of Dylan, last met with Dylan two years ago, when Dylan was still living in Greenwich Village, and had taken an interest in Scaduto's book. Scaduto, now completing a book on Mick Jagger, got a free ticket and watched the subject of his book through 7 x 35 binoculars Thursday night. "It was outrageous," he said. "I'm not really a Dylan freak, but for me this was the most outrageous thing since the Stones in '69, just before Altamont."

Was there a homecoming feeling to Dylan's concert in New York? "Yes," Scaduto said, "there was a feeling he was performing for *his* people." The local CBS station, Scaduto said, did a three-part series on Dylan for its 11 o'clock news, and gathered some of Dylan's old Village buddies, among them Dave Van Ronk, at whose home Dylan stayed when he first hit New York, and Barry Kornfield, musician and record producer. Scaduto's summary: "Everyone seemed to be creating the feeling that . . . Bobby's home."

Dylan, in his recent interview with ROLLING STONE (February 14th), suggested that New York would still be his home, that Malibu was only a weather-wise stopover, after his role in *Pat Garrett and Billy the Kid*. "I can't stay away from New York!" he'd declared.

But even though it was clearly a homecoming, 14 years since his arrival and soar to fame here—almost two years since he drifted off to Mexico for the movie and then up to Malibu—the Village folkies who came to see him were outnumbered by the pop and political stars attending opening night, Wednesday, January 30th, at Madison Square Garden.

Almost from the start of the tour, in Chicago, January 3rd, there had been rumors about a "superstar jam" in New York, the likely jammers being the four ex-Beatles, Leon Russell, Mick Jagger, and a few other "friends." As it happened, the only jam that took place was in the aisles, before showtime, as common folks stopped to gawk at the likes of Yoko Ono and Maureen Starkey (without their husbands), Carly Simon, James Taylor, Paul Simon, Johnny Winter, Dick Cavett, Shirley MacLaine, Jack Nicholson and John Kennedy, Jr.

(Another opening-night, offstage star, Bette Midler, returned to see a second show the next day; later, after attending a quiet party for Dylan and the Band at the St. Moritz hotel, she reported to a friend: "He's just fabulous. I even pinched his ass.")

Some of the people who were close to Dylan in the early Sixties were also at opening night. They included Mike Porco, original owner of Gerde's Folk City, where Dylan first performed in the Village, on Monday audition nights; it was Porco who hired Dylan for the stay in September, 1961, that drew Robert Shelton from *The New York Times* and resulted in the review that led to his recording contract with Columbia. Along with Porco, there was Mary Travers, whose group, Peter, Paul and Mary, brought mass attention to Dylan by recording "Blowin' in the Wind." And Marjorie Guthrie and her daughter Nora. Marjorie Guthrie first saw Dylan, in 1961, as a charming, "odd-looking boy" who'd come to her doorstep in Queens, looking to visit her dying husband, his idol, Woody Guthrie. And there was Allen Ginsberg and Happy and Artie Traum.

Happy and Artie are folk fixtures in New York—writers, composers, guitar teachers, and performing artists. Happy, with John Cohen, did the excellent interview with Dylan in *Sing Out* in late 1968, then sang harmony on a couple of tracks that ended up in Dylan's *Greatest Hits, Volume 2* album: "I Shall Be Released" and "You Ain't Goin' Nowhere." He visited with Dylan at Dylan's hotel, the Plaza, after the concert, and both Traums were invited to the St. Moritz party, but they chose to go back to Woodstock instead. (The party, intended as a gathering of Dylan's old friends, was, like opening night, dominated by celebrities, including Art Garfunkel, Cavett, Midler, Nicholson, and several music-biz moguls. Like the few other parties on the tour, this one was small and sober.) Later, we reached Artie Traum. Artie used to have to sneak into Gerde's (because he was underage) to see Dylan and liked Dylan for the "emotional quality about his performances" and for his long, humorous talks between numbers. At Madison Square—Traum's first time at a "big concert," he said—he was on his feet at the end of the show, "clapping along with all the teenyboppers."

He was surprised by his own reaction, he said. "When it started, the first three or four songs, I didn't like it, and then I realized why. I had expectations, and it occurred to me that if I'd just hear it as what it was—I got into it, and I thought it was fantastic."

Still, Traum missed the Dylan of the Gerde's days. "I felt there was no emotion in the concert," he said. "It was powerful in a certain way. And there was some kind of emotion, maybe it was anger that I felt, which is very powerful, but maybe there was a lack of gentleness. But I'm afraid it really would have wiped people out, because those are the most powerful songs. Other than that, I was knocked out."

Tony Scaduto also saw Dylan, first at Gerde's, in Dylan's first paid performance, opening for John Lee Hooker. "He was terrible, trying to sing like a black man,"

Scaduto said. "I turned onto him when he went electric." At the Madison Square show Thursday night, Scaduto saw a Dylan in much more control than he was during the 1965–1966 tour with the Band (then the Hawks). "The manic edge from back then was gone," he said. For Scaduto, the concert "worked marvelously, the new interpretations. Let's see: On 'Gates Of Eden' he was singing almost as if he was reading from the Bible. 'Baby Blue,' going through it quickly, like he was reading *The New York Times,* you know, saying, 'We've gone through all this before.' "

Dylan's three concerts at Madison Square Garden were recorded by Phil Ramone, the engineer who previously recorded the Band's *Rock Of Ages,* from the Academy of Music concerts that featured a visit from Dylan on New Year's Eve, 1971. For *Rock Of Ages,* Ramone had been warned not to expect much rehearsing from the Band; this time, he had all of a ten-minute sound check at 5:00 PM opening night. The session was kept short so that the musicians could be fresh for the first concert.

According to Geffen, concerts in Los Angeles, San Francisco, and Seattle were also going to be recorded, and a live album would be released—possibly as early as April, but only if the recordings were "really great," not just good. Meantime, *Planet Waves* shot to Number One on the Billboard album charts, just two weeks after release. While Dylan has received 12 gold albums, he had never reached the top spot before. Once again, while Dylan himself is avoiding publicity, forces around him seem to be doing their work.

In New York, media center of the country, Dylan granted no interviews. Reporters representing ABC and CBS had been jostling for position, but Dylan remained sheltered. The only media breakthrough was scored by WNBC-TV, whose crew somehow slipped by the guards at Nassau Coliseum and shot portions of Dylan's acoustic set. The footage was aired on the station's parent network, NBC, on two newscasts and on the "Today" show. Filming of Dylan had been forbidden, according to Geffen, and at press time, he was still threatening legal action against WNBC.

At Madison Square Garden, all security was calm. Outside, local promoter Ron Delsener, who worked with Graham, said security on surrounding streets was as beefed up as for, say, a Rolling Stones or Led Zeppelin concert, but no more. Neither the promoter nor the Garden would give information on just how many guards were stationed, but wooden-sawhorse barricades were set up to screen out nonticketholders and possible gatecrashers. We passed through three guards at three different points before being admitted. Inside, it was the usual complement of cops, guards, and ushers for a rock concert. Audiences complied with Graham's request to keep aisles clear; a few people crept up near the stage to take a snapshot, but immediately went back to their seats. As Graham said, "They don't want to conquer that terrain. This is not a physical dexterity contest." Joe Cohen, a Madison Square Garden employer, said that there were fewer security personnel inside the Garden than there were at the Ali-Frazier superfight.

At the Garden, Jim Farber, 16, of Hartsdale, New York, sat in the third row. "I want to grab Dylan's respect," he said. "I don't want him to think that I'm a teenybopper. I want him to feel that his audience is intelligent."

The only foul-up in New York was over tickets. Madison Square Garden announced, two weeks before the concerts, that they had several thousand tickets for sale, through city-wide Ticketron box offices, this after the announcement, in early December, that the Garden had received 20 requests for every seat they had and were returning tens of thousands of checks. The Garden, according to Graham, simply assumed that each envelope would contain requests for four tickets. Opening the envelopes, a month later, they discovered many requests for only one or two tickets, and announced the availability of tickets. The move angered thousands who had rushed their mail orders in and been refused. As Graham put it: "They say, 'Ticketron?! I took my envelope at 12:01 to the main post office. I spoke to my rabbi. I waited every day for my mailman. Now they're putting them in Ticketron!' It was so stupid and ugly. But it was their fuck-up."

Still, Graham, as tour producer, was ultimately responsible. "That's why I get these calls. 'Mr. Graham, I always had faith in you, and then you do *this* to me.' I should have stayed a waiter."

The Bob Dylan tour winds up on St. Valentine's Day at the Forum, where it all began seven weeks before, with the first formal rehearsal of Bob Dylan and the Band.

SCALPERS ALSO SAW THE TOUR

Ticket scalpers were as plentiful as suckerfish on a shark in some cities along the 1974 Bob Dylan tour, expected to net $2.5 million. And as the tour neared its climax in Los Angeles, it appeared the scalpers, too, had made a profit.

In New York, San Francisco, and Los Angeles—where mail-order tickets had been virtually an instant sellout—a seat was worth from $15 to $75 on the street. The average scalper's price—as best as could be determined in talks with concert-goers, rock radio-station switchboard operators, auditorium managers and scalpers—was $25–$30.

Most of those who obtained inflated prices—street hustlers, send-money-Dad college students, or simply persons unable to attend shows for personal reasons—appeared to be acting individually.

However, in Ann Arbor, Michigan, a promotion agency was accused of involvement in a scheme to place 300–1000 tickets on the black market, where they sold for $15–$75. The University of Michigan *Daily,* in a copyrighted story, said the scalping operation involved choice, main-floor seats for the February 2nd show at Crisler Arena.

Promoting the concert was Bamboo Enterprises of Detroit. The firm was hired by Bill Graham's FM Productions to coordinate Ann Arbor ticket sales with the university, a co-promoter.

When the concert ended Graham took the microphone and asked the audience of 13,600 for help in finding the people "who knew how it was done." Graham told a reporter for the *Daily* there had been "obvious hanky-panky."

In New York, Joe Cohen, director of development at Madison Square Garden, said the mail-order ticket procedure there had mitigated a lot of street scalping. (However, another source said there were a few tickets going for $25.) Cohen said the Rolling Stones shows in 1972 generated much more scalping. But neither event could compare with the first Ali-Frazier heavyweight fight, when $150 ringside seats were scalped for $1000, he said.

At San Francisco State University, one student sold several tickets for $50 by advertising on bulletin boards. However, by showtime, a scalper outside the Oakland Coliseum Arena was asking a mere $20, and you got the impression he'd come down.

The Poet's Poet

By Michael McClure

Memory is a beautiful thing—as I get older I learn to cherish it. It seems so beautiful or ugly that it is often more than real. Sometimes the vision is lit up with imagination; sometimes the imaginings have the shapes of real acts and gestures we call experience.

Experience is physical matter—and there is no sense in hanging onto it. It is a pleasure to let memory pour through the consciousness like nuggets of gold and moss agates and crystals of quartz clicking through the fingers at a rock shop. One never plans to keep those stones but the pleasure of feeling them is lovely.

The autoharp Bob Dylan gave me early in 1966 sat on the mantelpiece for six weeks before I picked it up and strummed it. A black and magical autoharp. Afraid of music, I had always felt totally unmusical—except in appreciation. Bob had asked me what instrument I'd like to play. (I was writing song lyrics.) I said autoharp out of the clear blue though I had no picture of what an autoharp looked like. There must have been people playing them on farms in my Kansas childhood.

San Francisco poets were poor in 1965 and it was an impressive present and it committed me to music. There was the interest in writing lyrics and perhaps a new way to use rhyme.

Rock had mutual attraction for all; a common tribal dancing ground whether we were poets, or printers, or sculptors, it was a form we all shared. I spent a year and a half learning to play autoharp in an eccentric way and wrote songs like "The Blue Lyon Laughs," "The Allen Ginsberg for President Waltz," and "Come on God, and Buy Me a Mercedes Benz."

I bought an old amplifier and stood in front of the mirror whanging on the autoharp. Obsessed with John Keats' question—What weapon has the lion but himself—I tried to make it a song and sang it so many times so loudly that I wonder what the neighbors thought in those old days when acid rock was a baby.

In December, 1965, when we had been bombing Vietnam for eight months, Dylan read "Poisoned Wheat," a long antiwar poem of mine. One day as we were eating chicken, I handed him another copy. He left huge greasy fingerprints and he did it with complete aplomb. It seemed very non-materialistic and natural not to notice the blotches. It seemed right to treat works of art as part of the transformations of life. Later I gave the copy to a girl who wanted Bob's fingerprints.

The first person to play a Dylan album for me was poet David Meltzer. It was Dylan's first album, and I heard it shortly after it came out in March or April of 1962. I could not understand what David heard in the album. In high school I knew people at the University of Chicago and in New York City who were singing like that—just some hillbilly-intellectual music that I'd gotten bored with earlier. In retrospect, Dylan must have shown a direct creative thrust without the "Art" self-consciousness of other singers.

Early in 1965 a friend of my wife Joanna came to visit and brought the Dylan album with "She Belongs to Me." The album had changed her life-image from a tragic loser to a proud artist. Joanna heard and understood Dylan at once and completely, I think.

In 1965 everyone had been after me to listen to Dylan carefully—to sit down and listen to the words *and* the music. I absolutely did *not* want to hear Dylan. I imagined, without admitting it to myself, that Dylan was a threat to poetry—or to my poetry. I sensed that a new mode of poetry, or rebirth of an old one, might replace my mode. In the long run, rock lyrics have sensitized many people to words and brought them to discover poetry.

At last I could not resist Joanna's demand that I hear the album. We had a banged-up record player in the hallway at the top of the stairs. Later at night, in the pale-gray hallway light, Joanna sat me down in front of the speaker and told me to listen to the words. I began to hear what the words were saying, not just the jangling of the guitar and the harmonica and the whining nasal voice. The next thing I knew I was crying. It was "Gates Of Eden": "At dawn my lover comes to me/And tells me of her dreams/With no attempts to shovel the glimpse/Into the ditch of what each one means. . . ."

I had the idea that I was hallucinating, that it was William Blake's voice coming out of the walls and I stood up and put my hands on the walls and they were vibrating.

Then I went back to those people who had tried to get me to listen and I told them that I thought the revolution had begun. "Gates Of Eden" and those other songs seemed to open up the post-Freudian and postexistentialist era. Everyone didn't have to use the old explanations and the mildewed rationalities any longer.

By the time I met Bob, his poetry was important to me in the way that Kerouac's writing was. It was not something to imitate or be influenced by; it was the expression of a unique individual and his feelings and perceptions.

There is no way to second-guess poetry or to predict poetry or to convince a poet that the very best songs in the world are poetry if they are not. Bob Dylan is a poet; whether he has cherubs in his hair and fairy wings, or feet of clay, he is a poet. Those other people called "rock poets," "song poets," "folk poets," or whatever the rock critic is calling them this week, will be better off if they are appreciated as songwriters.

At a party after his concert at the Berkeley Community Theatre in December, 1965, Dylan told me that he had not read Blake and did not know the poetry. That seemed hard to believe so I recited a few stanzas: One was the motto to "The Songs of Innocence and Experience" which begins: "The Good are attracted by Men's perceptions/ And think not for themselves/Till Experience teaches them to catch/And to cage the Fairies & Elves. . . ."

Bob was sitting on the floor and everyone crowded around him. Joanna, who has a tendency to go to sleep when she's pleased and in a crowd, started to sleep with her head in my lap. Someone told her in an ugly way that she ought to wake up—that if she didn't want to hear what was being said, there were plenty of others who would like her place close to Dylan. One wonders if those were honors being paid to a popular poet, or a worshipful voice in the crowd that the poet argues against.

In 1965 that first Dylan concert in the Bay Area was at the Masonic Auditorium. In those days the Masonic seemed huge and rather plush. It was the first time I'd heard Bob Dylan in person. The records were beautiful but this was better—an immaculate performance with inflections or nuances different from the albums. Dylan was purest poet. Like an elf being, so perfect was he and so ferocious in his persistence for perfection. There was a verge of anger in him waiting for any obstacle to the event.

After the Masonic Auditorium concert we went to the Villa Romano Motel, where Bob and the Hawks were staying, and met Al Grossman. He, Joan Baez, Allen Ginsberg, and I spoke for a while. Joan said that Allen and I should be Bob's conscience. It seemed a beautiful thing to say, though not clear at the time. Later Joan wrote that we should hold Bob in our consciousness.

A night or two later, after another concert, there was a party for Bob in San Francisco. Ken Kesey bounced through the door with a few of his Merry Pranksters. Ruddy with the vigor of good health, Los Gatos sunshine

and acid, Kesey immediately hit Dylan with something like, "Hey, man, you should try playing while you're high on acid." Without a pause Dylan said, "I did and it threw off my timing." There was no way to one-up Bob or to get ahead of him at any level or any time. You knew that pop stars like Dylan or Lennon drove around in black cars and they were careful and they were very fast and they were staying where they were and they were not kidding.

Nine years later, on the plane going to Dylan's Philadelphia concert, I reread Robert Duncan's small book, *Seventeenth Century Suite.* Duncan has vowed not to commercially publish any of his new poetry for 15 years, so that no pressure would direct him to write anything other than what he wishes most deeply. By canceling formal publication he was essentially vowing to please only himself. Robert made an edition of 200 copies of *Seventeenth Century Suite* and gave them to friends for Christmas gifts.

How incredibly far it is from Duncan's private edition of *Seventeenth Century Suite* to Dylan's millions of albums. Both are fine poetry and though they seem poles apart, they almost touch in their subtle images and music. One can imagine the radiance and spectrum of the poetry in between.

It is a mistake to wonder which poetry will matter 30 years from now. We should wonder what is wrong if Dylan's songs do not mean something to us today. We are all moved by spiritual experiences. For some of us the spiritual experiences can be the grossest hit songs or the most kitsch painting. It is really a matter of whether we are ogres or elves—or something in between drawn one way or the other at one moment and another.

The Philadelphia concert made the Masonic Auditorium of San Francisco 1965 seem like a jam session in a small nightclub. The crowd was not in their late 20s and early 30s as friends in San Francisco had predicted—this was an audience of nice-looking, scruffy young people in their early 20s. The tri-sexuals and glitter bunnies were obvious by their absence. All in all, except for the number of bodies (making one think of the pictures of a Tokyo beach), one did not mind being there. There were some of the best people around, a part of the backbone of the future—the people with hope and some enthusiasm in a country run over for eight years by the War Machine.

The lights went down accompanied by a burst of enthusiasm from the 19,000 living souls.

To open the first set houselights came down into darkness very fast. Colored spotlights flashed to the stage and banks of colored lights shone. The Band and Bob Dylan almost ran onstage and began playing without a pause while the audience was still cheering their enthusiasm.

There were two thoughts that someone had imparted to me. One was that Bob was doing his old songs as rock for the new rock generation who did not know him well. The second was that Dylan was in danger of disappearing into his own creation; that as one of the founders of the giant rock scene he had spawned so many followers, imitators, and Dylan-influenced groups and movements that he stood in danger of blending in among his own offspring and hybrids—ending up in the public eye as another surviving folk-rocker.

Dylan a grown man . . . a young man still, but a man. The elfish lightness of foot is gone and the perfection of timing is replaced by sureness; the nasal boy's voice replaced by a man's voice.

Another poet's singing came to mind: Allen Ginsberg at the 1966 Human Be-In singing his strange "Peace in America—Peace in Vietnam." Ginsberg introduced me to Dylan in 1965.

Now Dylan is official culture—like Brecht and Weill. He played "Mr. Jones"—in 1965 a glove thrown in the public face, a statement of revolt; now it is Art.

I could not take my eyes off the lights, hypnotized by the spots of amber, lavender, blue, red that kept playing on Dylan. The banks of lights up above the bandstand stage to the right and left kept bleeding and blinking off and on in time with the drama and melody of the songs. Bright lights kept popping in the blackness—intensely bright and silvery white in their flash. Flashbulbs! It seemed crazy that anyone sitting three blocks from the bandstand in darkness would be setting off flashbulbs. It seemed demented.

"My God, it is a long way since the Avalon Ballroom," I thought. A long way since the lightshows by Tony Martin and Bruce Conner and the smallness of the dance floors and the tribal dancers of 1966. We felt so crowded together, transpersonal, and magical in those days. In Philadelphia what I saw was gigantic! The incredible subtlety of the earlier lightshows was surpassed by the blending of colors, the motility of the spotlights, and sheer candlepower. The devastating volume of the music made it unpleasant trying to pick Dylan's words out of the roar. One became aware that the enormous volume of the amplified music mimicked, as it bounced off the walls, the roar of the crowd. The music became a response to itself. The effect would trigger in the audience a response to the music. Loud cheering. When it happened I wondered if that was entertainment or ethological manipulation—or if entertainment could be ethological manipulation.

I loved what I could hear of Dylan's new love songs—they seemed inspired. The melodies, lost in the amplified blare, were not impressive but I was able to hear: "May you always stay courageous/Be forever young. . . ."

In the darkness at the end of the concert, the audience lit matches and cigarette lighters, making a Milky Way of wavering lights and cheers—a universe of tiny flaming stars.

If a scholar goes seriously into an analysis of the poetry convergent with the rock movement there will be interesting contrasts between Lennon, Kerouac, Dylan and Ginsberg. The whole thing started with the poets of the Fifties. It was an alchemical-biological movement, not a literary one. An English group with shiny jackets called the Silver Beetles took Jack Kerouac's word "Beat," grew their hair out and became The Beatles. It was beautiful! Bob Dylan's "Dylan" is from Dylan Thomas, the Welsh poet so popular in the Fifties. Allen Ginsberg asked if I'd heard that Dylan was titling his album *Planet Waves*. I asked Allen what he thought of that. Allen said, "Charming! Delightful! Great!"

I think so too. Allen's last book was *Planet News*. There's plenty of room for feedback back and forth.

At the Toronto concert, Marshall McLuhan and his wife were in the audience. McLuhan told me that he had played Dylan albums to a poetry class that morning. McLuhan believes that rock & roll comes out of the English language—using its rhythms and inflections as a basis for melody. (Exactly what I believe—and also that it comes out of the Beat mutation or has the same root.) The future of rock, he felt, would be the same as that of the language; that it would have ups and downs as the language does.

As a mode, the ballad and story-song seem mined-out, I said. Anyone can write a story-song in almost any manner and it becomes uninteresting to listen to. McLuhan felt it is the background, not the mode, that gives out. The background is violence, and Dylan was singing violently. "Violence is the result of a loss of identity—the more loss the greater the violence."

Sitting among 19,000 people McLuhan said, "Gravity is like acoustic space—the center is everywhere."

I told Marshall that I wanted to go out into the hallway in the last set of the concert when Dylan and the Band played "Like a Rolling Stone." The night before I had been carried away and wept so hard that I did not want to have the experience again. This was my third concert and the incredible volume of the speakers was beginning to undermine my nerves.

I first heard "Like a Rolling Stone" when Joanna and I were driving in an open MG across the Arizona-California desert with our daughter curled up asleep behind us next to our Russian wolfhound and our pet black-and-white rat sleeping in his cage on the floor of the sports car. The moon was on the horizon. A song never hit me so hard except as a child when my mother sang to me. Much of our poetic sensibility may have its origins with cradle songs—I remember my mother singing songs from Disney cartoons and movies and reciting Mother Goose.

Dylan sang well, putting on extra temperament, and I

wondered if he consciously or unconsciously put force behind his lines about professors and critics.

After the concert there was a moment to introduce McLuhan and his wife to Bill Graham and Barry Imhoff and Dylan before Bob and the Band went back onstage for their encore.

Pouring sweat, his face puffy, his eyes partially blanked by the concert he'd just delivered, Bob smiled as much as he could. In the auditorium almost 20,000 people were screaming and yelling for him to come back so he could reconnect them briefly to the godhead.

When Dylan and the Band ran back onstage, Marshall said that this was his first rock concert. Graham replied: "I wish I could say the same thing!" Bill had been concerned because everything was going too well. There is a theater superstition that if small things don't go wrong then something major will.

Dylan has slipped into people's dream baskets. He has been incorporated into their myths and fantasies. They worry about him: whether he is understood, what his next album will be like, if he is appreciated by the press, whether he might get a cold, and how he performs his pieces.

My particular fantasy is that he is underpaid. I would not stand in front of 20,000 people and those lights and amplifiers and do what he is doing for all the dollars in the world or for a stack of gold records.

Bob is a prisoner of his fame and fortune. When he says, "I'm anyone who lives in a vault, . . ." he means himself. He is a real poet who lives the poems that he sings. A lot of people who hold Dylan in their dream baskets think the songs are a confection—that they are cute and sweet the way Rod McKuen is. But everything I've seen convinces me that Bob is the real thing, that he is no joke, that he has no answers, that he is a poet, that he is trapped most of the time.

The several new songs that I heard in the concerts were domestic (about wife and home) and inspirational. I hope this is the direction that Dylan is going. It would be good to see lots of young Americans put back on their feet—not through renewed faith in the old values that have been shot down, but through greater awareness of themselves on an earth that was once beautiful—and that still has pockets of beauty. I'd like everyone to begin to get some sense of what, and who, they are—and a further sense that something can be done to elevate the vicious mindlessness of politics and bio-environmental destruction and the extinction of the species of living plants and animals. A lot of the poets are moving in that direction—Ginsberg, Snyder, Duncan, Creeley, Waldman.

Thinking of Dylan's poetics I had brought along some books as background material: *Seventeenth Century Suite* by Robert Duncan, poems by Gary Snyder and Allen Ginsberg, *Black Music* by Imamu Amiri Baraka (LeRoi Jones) and Kafka's "Josephine the Singer."

In *Black Music,* published in 1968, Baraka says that the content of white-rock, antiwar and antiauthoritarian songs generalizes "passionate luxurious ego demonstrations"; that the artists want to prove that they are good humans though in fact, Baraka contends, they are really sensitive antennae of the brutalized and brutalizing white social mass. Baraka insists that is a cop-out and the music is still wealthy white kids playing around. We should remember Baraka's viewpoint; it may be narrow but light sometimes passes through a thin slit. The Beatles did not write antiwar songs. When asked about that they replied that all their songs are against war. There may be some beams of light in that crack too.

In Toronto I read Kafka's "Josephine the Singer."* A mouse-narrator relates an account of a woman mouse named Josephine who is a singer. She proclaims herself a great artist and the other mice congregate to hear her at the risk of their lives. But nothing will satisfy her ambition. She has a coterie of worshipful followers. Many of the mice people, however, are not at all sure that what she does, as fascinating and important to them as it is, is sing-

---

* *The Penal Colony,* Franz Kafka, translated by Willa and Edwin Muir, Schocken Books, copyright, ©, 1948, by Schocken Books.

ing. They think that it may only be "piping" and perhaps it is her childishness (as she reflects simple attitudes of her people back to them) that is attractive: "Here is someone making a ceremonial performance out of the usual thing." Josephine demands freedom from the labor quota of the mouse people. But no matter how much they love or worship her they will not free her from the work law. Josephine disappears—perhaps has gone into hiding—to force people to accept her demands. Anyone interested in Dylan and/or poetry should look at the piece.

I thought of the creation of a demigod and prophet that took place in the multicolored spotlights and amplification and banks of stagelights—better known to the modern world than Plato or Confucius or Buddha; watched by thousands with millions wishing to see him in other cities. One can become a statue of one's self, mimicking what one is in eternity. Immortality (or its substitute) can be turned off and on and directed by voice over wires and captured on disks of black plastic. There is the possibility that the background has swallowed up the object and that we are in the process of whiting-out. If so, I think we stand in need of it.

"Poetry, in a general sense, may be defined to be the expression of the imagination; and poetry is connate with the origin of man. Man is an instrument over which a series of external and internal impressions are driven, like the alternations of an ever-changing wind over an Aeolian lyre, which move it by their motion to ever-changing melody. But there is a principle within the human being, and perhaps within all sentient beings, which acts otherwise than in the lyre, and produces not melody alone, but harmony, by an internal adjustment of the sounds or motions thus excited to the impressions which excite them. . . ."

Said Shelley in 1821 in *A Defense of Poetry.*

Like a Rolling Stone, Again

By Ralph J. Gleason

It took courage, after those six or eight or nine years, for Bob Dylan to make his recent two-pronged public appearance—a new album and a nationwide tour.

Yet artistic courage is exactly what Bob Dylan has been about in the 13 years since he hit Gerde's Folk City, with his tousled hair, Minnesota iron-ore twang and a head full of music.

Nelson Algren once said about Ernest Hemingway something which also fits the Dylan achievement: "No American writer since Walt Whitman has assumed such risks in forming a style. They were the kind of chances by which, should they fail, the taker fails alone; yet, should they succeed, succeed for everyone."

Dylan took the chances. He opened the minds of the American audience to the possibilities of poetry and music and he freed the whole of American pop music from the restraints of the music hall, the Broadway show and Tin Pan Alley. In the wake of the chances he took has come a new generation of song poets—some good, some bad—

but none who would have hopefully taken step one had not Dylan made the first move.

Dylan was faced with a serious dilemma when planning this tour. He must have wondered if he was out of touch. With each of his phases of development over the years he has simultaneously attracted a new audience and outraged elements of the previous one.

In the beginning, he was a folk singer with the standard coffeehouse repertoire plus some variations. He began his career as a "contemporary folk singer"—despite the apparent contradiction in terms. They were not old songs exactly, though the melody was generally traditional or at least derivative. Dylan sang them accompanied only by his own guitar and harp. But the lyrics were mostly new and they spoke of events which were contemporary.

Toward the end of that period of Dylan's career which produced "A Hard Rain's A-Gonna Fall," "The Times They Are A-Changin'," "Blowin' in the Wind," "Who Killed Davey Moore?," "With God on Our Side," and "The Lonesome Death of Hattie Carroll," Dylan began to drop into his albums and his concerts some other sides of his creative inspiration, songs such as "One Too Many Mornings," "Don't Think Twice, It's All Right," "It Ain't Me, Babe," and "It's All Over Now, Baby Blue." They were songs at the least about liaisons, just as "To Ramona," "Boots of Spanish Leather," and "Girl from the North Country" were flat-out love songs.

The political songs and the two kinds of love songs continued, though evolving, until his accident and the subsequent *John Wesley Harding* album. The love song became more rare, the liaison song went all the way to the anguish of "Positively 4th Street" before it, along with the political song, joined in a new Dylan series: the prophetic doomsday messages, State of the Union poems. They were vocal tears of rage and they defined the image of the American culture.

Out of the political songs and from those Gothic collections of eerie imagery, Dylan's audience extracted a view of the world—the world at hand, the USA—and a poetic and aesthetic rationale that bordered on religion.

His first audience, the folk music followers, went along partway because of the power of his imagery and of his political songs. They stayed with him until he plugged into the main current of American musical thought, picked up an electric band, and started a musical riot at the 1965 Newport Folk Festival by appearing onstage with the Paul Butterfield Blues Band.

Right then, the politicos and their contingent traditional folkie audience turned on him. The others, whom he had picked up with the shattering poetry of his newer work, stayed with him. The controversy went on with the intensity of today's argument over him, except that the forums were small and obscure. But the temperature of the battle was just as high. He was booed at Newport and when he went on tour with his new electric band—those sublime musicians who are now the Band—at Forest Hills, Minneapolis and elsewhere. Bob Dylan seldom appeared, in that last year (1966), at any concert in the US or Europe at which some disgruntled former fan did not boo him for not being what the fan wanted him to be. Johnny Cash finally ended it with a letter to Broadside magazine saying, "Shut up and let him sing!"

All along Dylan warned he had nothing to live up to and "you shouldn't let other people get your kicks for you." In every interview I know of, as well as in his songs, Dylan stressed he did not consider himself a leader.

But his audience saw him as not only a prophet but also a leader. He had shown them how to see their own world in new terms. He had helped them reevaluate their own knowledge, redefine their own feelings, and had given them the rhetoric with which to express themselves. He had remade their world.

And that's what the problem was. His audience believed him like revealed religion, and held him personally responsible for what he sang, forgetting what D. H. Lawrence, among others, had said: "Never trust the artist, trust the tale."

Dylan was injured in a motorcycle accident in midsummer 1966 and then appeared in public on only two occasions, the Tribute to Woody Guthrie at Carnegie Hall in 1968 and the Isle of Wight Festival in 1969. (His other appearances, at the concert for Bangladesh, and at a St. Louis concert and the Brooklyn Academy of Music, both with the Band, were unannounced.)

His only contact with his public was a series of albums —*John Wesley Harding, Nashville Skyline, New Morning* and *Self-Portrait*—which seemed to increase in intensity the new resentment of his former fans.

Dylan had changed the sound of his musical accompaniment. No longer was there a rock band, but country musicians from Nashville. The Nashville sound was soft and his new songs had a surprising sweetness to them. It was a gentle return. The songs were different in emphasis.

Dylan's accident had happened just as he had almost single-handedly transformed pop music into an alternative educational system. But when he reestablished communications with his audience by releasing the new albums, his poetic emphasis was personal. To his surprise, probably, he found that once again his former listeners, at least a large portion of them, felt betrayed. He no longer supplied them with what they wanted. As he wrote in *Writings and Drawings,* "If I can't please everybody, I might as well not please nobody at all."

The hostility and hurt that greeted his albums since the accident, in print and in coffeehouse discussions, have been the screams of outraged lovers. To be honest, they tell us less about the artist than about his critics.

Sometimes it seems as if the American audience *wants* to be betrayed, to have its heroes fatally flawed, and commands them to self-destruct.

But it is the artist, not the audience, who defines, in the end, the artist's role. His only responsibility is to himself and to his art. He has, truly, nothing to live up to. Like a poem, he *is*. You take it or you leave it alone. It makes no difference, there is only, at the bottom, as he once wrote me, ". . . no understanding of anything. At best, just winks of the eye . . ."

Forms are chosen by poets because the most important part of what they have to say seems to go better with that form than any other . . . and then, in its turn, the form develops and shapes the poet's imagination.

—W. H. Auden

All of us, to a greater or lesser extent, have to prepare to listen to his new musical performances against the background of his tumultuous history, against the tension of his dialogue with the audience, and against *a priori* assumptions and wishful thinking of our own. Even though we know you can't go home again, every one of us often wants to do just that; go back to a simpler time when there was love and trust and hope.

What did we get?

We got two of the most memorable musical events I have ever attended. Dylan's two Oakland concerts with the Band were gems of the performing arts. His studied casualness, his determined anti-show-business presence, was still there, though now he was no longer nervous. Whereas in the old days he had chattered nervously, telling short anecdotes and cracking jokes to cover his interminable guitar-tuning or the soaking of his harmonicas in water, now he went straight at it. Proud—to be sure—strong and in total command.

"It was a lesson in simplicity," a friend of mine commented. And it was a chance in this time of gay and glittering rock.

Dylan and the Band opened each show with a set of six songs, then Dylan returned for three more and, leaning abruptly to the microphone, said: "Don't go away. We'll be right back."

The second half opened with a five-song acoustic set by Dylan alone followed by four songs by the Band alone. Then Dylan returned and, in a final set of four songs with the Band, roared to a climax that left the audience shivering and screaming for more.

The Band has never played better in person or on record. They were hard-driving, rocking, swinging accompaniments for Dylan and majestic performances on their own. Robbie Robertson played guitar obbligatos or fills when Dylan was singing that compared in emotional intensity and artistic simplicity to Louis Armstrong behind Bessie Smith. Within the total sound of the band, a pulsing, cracking, shaking sound, there was an infinity of variety and internal musical activity.

There's something which ought to be said right away about the Band and this tour. This is the largest concert tour they have ever been on in terms of numbers of people in the audience. They performed so brilliantly in Oakland—and, from all reports, everywhere they played—that I would expect they could now go out and do almost as well alone. Especially if the new album Robbie is working on has an impact, in terms of new material, comparable to what they did on this tour. The Band has really come out front with the larger audience. I think they can now do whatever they want and I hope it includes more tours with Dylan.

Dylan was in amazing form. This had been a long and tiring tour, despite every care taken by Bill Graham to make it as easy on the musicians as possible. But they rose above any physical limitations and they took the crowd with them. Dylan smiled and executed a series of bows that resembled a 17th Century cavalier doffing his plumed hat with one hand and leaning on his sword with the other.

The songs that Dylan did with the Band were nearly all new in a musical sense. They all now had different tempos, new kickoffs, new arrangements, sometimes new melodic lines and new keys and new endings.

Dylan's voice is stronger now. Very sure and very flexible. Surrounded by the overwhelming energy of the Band with Robbie's guitar whipping and cracking behind it, Dylan sometimes used his voice itself like an electric guitar, screaming and soaring and changing the sound of the words by that trick of appearing to smile by the way he pronounces words.

The result of all of this was overwhelming. When he came on to open the first show, a young friend of mine said in tones of wonder, "God damn! It's really *him!*" and at the end of the night, two young men sat in the orchestra determinedly clapping 20 minutes after the end of the show, the sound of their hands echoing throughout the huge arena.

I went back to the album, *Planet Waves,* though the concert had not exactly faded from my memory (it will be a long time before that happens) and I found in it, as has so often been the case with Dylan's work, even more things than I had at first.

Dylan has by now created his own musical and poetic rhetoric which stands on its own as a vehicle for his work, much the same as Duke Ellington. True, there are occasional touches here and there of other times and other people, but it has all been absorbed, recycled and utilized again in a dramatically personal way.

There is a further point about the lyrics. It seems rather unlikely when he was growing up in Hibbing that Dylan absorbed his seminal influences in imagery, allusion and poetry by listening exclusively to Gatemouth Moore's nightly Little Rock broadcasts of American popular music, rich in the blues language though they may have been. In addition to listening, Dylan obviously read voraciously. Thus it might be that he came across and took literally Rimbaud's dictum: "The poet makes himself a seer, by long, prodigious and rational disordering of the senses. Every form of love, of suffering, of madness; he searches himself, he consumes all the poisons in him and keeps only their quintessence. This is an unspeakable torture during which he needs all his faith and the superhuman strength and during which he becomes the great patient, the great criminal, the great accursed—and the great learned one among men. For he drives at the *unknown!* Because he has cultivated his own soul—which was rich to begin with —more than any other man! He reaches the unknown and even if, crazed, he ends up by losing the understanding of his visions, at least he has seen them! Let him die charging through these unutterable, unnameable things: other horrible workers will come: they will begin from the horizons where he has succumbed! . . . The poet really is the thief of fire . . . [and] eternal art will have its function, since poets are citizens. Poetry will no longer rhyme with action; it will be ahead of it."

But Dylan, untrue to Rimbaud's prophecy, did not succumb. He survived the torture of the road, the accident and all the shit that has gone down since then. He has returned to us now with a fuller, more developed art. He always wrote love songs, but they were overshadowed by the political verse, despite the beauty and strength of songs like "Girl from the North Country," "Mama, You've Been on My Mind" and "To Ramona."

But for a time he did not. Once, during the period immediately after being booed at Newport and Forest Hills, he told a questioner, "I wish I could write like 'Girl from the North Country,' but I can't write like that any more. I dunno why." And then he denied there had been a change in his writing style. "When did I make the change? That was other people writing, you didn't hear anything from me. You know, I used to write a long time ago and it was almost the way I'm writing now."

I believe his love songs will survive above all else. Love is eternal, corny as that may sound. The polemics, for all the chains of flashing images and their ability to coalesce emotions and move the spirit, are, after all, often tied to the times in which they were written and these times are changing.

This new album is a collection of love songs interspersed with lines and phrases which, while not exactly asides, may be considered remarks upon Dylan's personal history.

This is, I tend to believe, the most musicianly of all Dylan's albums. His own playing and singing are of a high caliber, obviously a notch above all of his other efforts. He seems more sure of himself as a singer and I get the impression, from the musicianly things he does, that he has more fun with his voice now that he can use it like an instrument. On the last chorus of "Something There Is About You," Dylan sings that title phrase in a descending seven-note arpeggio, which he executes perfectly, in tune and with exquisite intonation.

Like the Band, Dylan knows what *not* to play or to sing. The hardest lesson of all to learn. The Band itself has done something only truly great musicians, secure in the knowledge of their own strengths, can do. They have sublimated themselves to the fellow artist and eschewed opportunity and temptation to forcefully step out. It is to their eternal credit. They are men, not boys. They know that nobody has to be heavy.

There is little over-dubbing on the album except for the occasional addition of the Band's voices and a few places where I hear a harp or guitar track laid down in addition to the basic take. It sounds as if it were done live—with the vocals recorded with the music—and in one or two takes. It has that special spontaneity about it.

Dylan's harp playing has always fascinated me. I have frequently thought of it as akin to Garth Hudson's organ introductions and interludes in complexity and humor.

The sound of the guitars is exquisitely recorded (applause for Rob Fraboni, the engineer), and the subtle interchanges and relationships between the various instruments indicate the highest level of professional skill (with the essential addition of the musicians' own love.)

Dylan says on the jacket that these are "Cast Iron Songs and Torch Ballads." "On a Night Like This" opens the program in an uptempo Texas bounce with echoes of Rosa's Cantina, perhaps. You can have this one either way. I find it a rollicking good-time song with some of the exuberance of "New Morning." It has amazing interplay between the harp and the accordion behind the vocal as well as some really exciting harp playing on the last chorus.

The second track, "Going, Going, Gone," brings the tempo down slow and Dylan's voice out front. It is a song of decision, "closing the book on the pages and the text; I don't really care, oooh, what happens next." The mood is somber, almost ghostly, akin to "Just Like Tom Thumb's Blues," as Robbie's guitar smears into a ringing minor howl after the third word in the title each time it is sung. The delicate and beautiful guitar work is present throughout. The juxtaposition of piano chords, guitar and organ sounds, like a kind of accompaniment to a silent film, effectively implies disaster and terror.

"Tough Mama" is a brawler, a Cast Iron song if ever there was one. It has the imagery of *Highway 61* and *Freewheelin'* and adds two more great lines which Dylan fans will be quoting: "I ain't haulin' any of my lambs to the market place any more" and "I gained some recognition but I lost my appetite!"

Throughout the album Dylan mixes love songs with bits of personal writing. Not only the romantic "Hazel" but also "Something There Is About You" has this touch. In other songs, such as "Dirge" and "Going, Going, Gone," he is frankly autobiographical, in the same way he was before the accident in those songs which first blew people's minds. He even sometimes has allusions to other Dylan songs such as the line in "Dirge" about "the Doom Machine," a flashback to the "heart attack machine" in "Desolation Row," and in "Never Say Goodbye," a North Country love song where he sings, "Oh baby, baby, baby blue, you've changed your last name too."

And there is "Something There Is About You," a most powerful love song with its echoes in the introductions to "The Weight" and "Spanish Harlem Incident." Despite the love song poetry, both in the descriptive passages and in the statements to his love who walks in mystery, yet moves with style and grace, there are direct personal statements: "I was in a whirlwind; now I'm in some better place," as well as the romantic recollections of his early days in northern Minnesota. The artist is talking about himself again, openly, nakedly and, I submit, poetically. He does it in "Wedding Song," which is a frank tribute to a lovely wife, when he sings:

It's never been my duty
To remake the world at large
Nor is it my intention
To sound a battle charge
'Cause I love you more than all of that
With a love that doesn't bend
And if there is eternity
I'd love you there again.*

* Ram's Horn Music/ASCAP.

The song is a poem of devotion and promise, of acceptance and recognition; a pure love song that has a line that all lovers must envy: "I love you more than ever and I haven't yet begun."

"Forever Young," as the last track of the first side, is done slowly and with infinite care. Again the guitars are particularly tastefully done with delicate sound. It is a song of good wishes, almost a prayer for happiness. The guitar at the head of the song seems an echo continued from the previous track, its mood fits so neatly.

"Forever Young" is repeated, to open side two, this time with an uptempo rockabilly accompaniment. Dylan sings it more harshly and eliminates the choruses, substituting a series of harp and accordion interludes. Its simplicity makes it seem offhand, but it certainly is not.

"Dirge" speaks directly to the whole Dylan history. The piano (played by Dylan à la "Ballad of a Thin Man") duets with the guitar in the intro and in the preface to each of the verses. The lyric lines are really memorable: "Go sing your praise of progress and of the Doom Machine, the naked truth is still taboo whenever it can be seen." Dylan seems somehow to be reaching for an explanation here, yet the times in which this song is heard do not yet allow the vision to be clear, an impossible task even for a visionary in the murky society of the moment.

"You Angel You" is a kind of crazy love song with some of the stream of consciousness stanzas of the past. There is more than one place here where, for a flash, it would be possible to carry the line of his voice and its sound off into another Dylan song. It is an eerie feeling.

"Wedding Song" is Dylan, concert style, alone, accompanied only by his own guitar. It is a pure love song, a poem of devotion and promise, of acceptance and recognition.

It is a fine album, well and truly done. It is eloquent, imaginative and, as always, good fun. This humor pops out all over the place, especially in his juxtaposition of light lines of common speech against obviously serious lines. Dylan, like any artist, by definition takes his work seriously, but I have never thought he took *himself* seriously, as there is too long a history of wry, almost offhand humor.

Dylan's true biography is his various writings. This album is an important chapter in that saga. It is characteristic of the Dylan songs that they grow on you and expand in meaning the more they are heard, as does any poem. Only "Subterranean Homesick Blues," "A Hard Rain's A-Gonna Fall" and "Like a Rolling Stone" had the quality of explosive immediate impact. The others took time to grow and groove. I find the new ones in the same mode: they grow and I change the one I think is my favorite, day by day.

Dylan went into the studio and laid it all down in three days. Only twice before in record history, to my knowledge, has an instant classic been done so quickly. Louis Armstrong did it in the Twenties with his Hot Five and Hot Seven with Kid Ory, Johnny and Baby Dodds. And then at the end of the Fifties, Miles Davis did it with a quintet that included John Coltrane and Philly Joe Jones.

You have to know what you are doing to bring that off. It separates the men from the boys. Dylan's deliberate simplicity—his decision not to use all the devices and electronic crutches available in the studio and, instead, to rely on the quality of the music itself—is a drastic and daring move.

Dylan Thomas, whose relationship to the poet under discussion is obvious, once said, "Poetry finds its own form; form should never be superimposed; the structure should rise out of the words and the expression of them."

To my ears this is exactly what Bob Dylan and the Band have done with this album and in the concerts. It is an achievement I am certain will stand the test of time.

Dylan: A Restful Farewell to Tour '74

By Ben Fong-Torres

If you looked hard enough you could trace the grin on Bob Dylan, watching, then politely, clop, clop, applauding a jelly-belly dancer Bill Graham had hired to entertain. He had also clapped for the strolling trio—two violinists and an accordion—that had serenaded during dinner, schmaltzing up to each table with love songs like "Fascination," "What Now, My Love" and "Somewhere My Love" on this Valentine's Day.

The scene was the crew dinner in Los Angeles, put together by Bill Graham for the 18 employees of his FM Productions. They had been in front of and behind Dylan and the Band—setting up and taking down the stage, sound, and lighting through 39 shows in 21 cities since January 3rd in Chicago. Now, at 7:45 P.M., the 39th show over only minutes before, they were gathered, along with Dylan and the Band, at the Forum Club, a banquet facility within the Fabulous Forum, home of L.A.'s basketball Lakers and hockey Kings. They were here, in this spread of rooms usually held for big businessmen/season ticket holders, for a quick round of roast beef and congratulations.

Graham kept the back-patting short. One quick speech thanking the crew and "the six great musicians" for doing their jobs so well. And, to each musician, a handshake and a memento: a wooden plaque, in the shape of a guitar, embossed with the signatures of Graham and the FM Productions crew.

The stringed strollers and the belly roller gave dinner a leisurely glow. But, in fact, the room was cleared within another hour. Just before nine, everyone—except for other special guests like the wives of the performers—was off to the backstage area. There was one more to go.

Before the first concert in Chicago, Bob Hilburn, the music columnist for the *Los Angeles Times,* kept elbowing and tugging at me. "Don't you feel the expectancy?" he asked repeatedly, awe-eyeing the crowd. "Don't you feel the excitement?" The most obvious excitement came from inside Hilburn, and that was fine. But the audiences, if any generalization could be made, were simply calm, ready for anything.

But in Los Angeles, it had to be different. If there were a hard-ticket show on the tour, this would be the one. Roger McGuinn, the Byrd who showed Dylan how his folk lyrics could be rocked, was unable to get a ticket at the last minute. The previous evening, Jerry Garcia, who'd seen the concert two days before in Oakland, was at the Forum box office. Someone, he said, had claimed his will-call ticket, and he was standing there, copyrighted "What, me bummed?" smile on his recently shaven face. He was hoping to get word in to Bill Graham. He never did.

At the final show, the Fabulous Forum, which is in Inglewood near the airport, was dotted with stars: Carole King, Ringo Starr, Neil Young, David Crosby, Helen Reddy, Eric Burdon, Ramblin' Jack Elliott, Richard ("Cheech") Marin, Dory Previn, Jack Nicholson, Warren Beatty and, off to the side, Joan Baez. Other celebs, at the first two shows, included Rick Nelson, Neil Diamond, Dan Hicks, Jackie DeShannon, and two of Dylan's

Village friends, now with him on Asylum Records: David Blue and Bob Neuwirth.

Joan Baez, once close to Dylan, prefers not to talk about him. "It always makes me feel miserable afterwards," she told me in San Francisco. She saw the second of the two Oakland concerts and kept relatively still, swaying gently with her arms folded through the lights-up hoedown finale, "Like a Rolling Stone." Tonight, she said, she'd dropped the expectations she'd carried into the Oakland Coliseum and seemed ready to roll with it. "You know, I like rock & roll."

The last show began at 9:30, with bassist/vocalist Rick Danko running onto the stage, sporting his J. C. Penney Glen-plaid jacket and jeans outfit, while Dylan, who usually ignored the welcoming ovation by becoming immediately immersed in tuning up and getting on with the show, let the guitar wait for a few seconds while he greeted the crowd, raising both arms and doing a little 360-degree twirl. It was clear that the artists smelled victory.

Two and a half hours later, at five after midnight, Dylan had done "Rolling Stone" and just about completed the show, structured just like most of the previous 39. It was evident that the music had tightened; that the Band's Danko and Richard Manuel had lost their singing voices; that Dylan continued to get looser with his re-reads of his classics, putting new italics into old songs—"*Ya* say yer lookin' for some*one*" . . . "It *still* ain't me, babe" . . . "You don't know what it is, do you, Mister *Jo*-hones" . . . and "You should be made to wear *tele*-phones."

Dylan offered more and fancier bows, front, rear, all around him. And even a new sign to replace the V and the fist. He formed circles with thumb and index finger—the old OK signal—and hoisted up both arms, Richard Nixon-style. He was doing it now, having played the encore, "Maggie's Farm," with the house lights still up from "Rolling Stone," and this should have been his departing gesture. But no, Dylan had one final surprise: He spoke to the audience for more than his usual one or two sentences (i.e., "Don't go away; we'll be right back!" and

"Good to be back in New York; you're a great audience," or "Good to be in Seattle, home of Jimi Hendrix!").

"We're gonna play one more," he announced, shouting out each part of each sentence. "But before we do, I'd like to introduce the man responsible for this tour! He's been behind the scene! Bill Graham!" A surprised Graham was hustled up to get his. Dylan shouted into the mike: "Barry Imhoff, too!" Imhoff, Graham's aide and tour coordinator, stepped out and wrapped an arm around Graham.

Dylan: "These guys put the show together! We couldn't have done it without them!" And he began the intro for "Blowin' in the Wind," rearranged into a bouncy, swaying little number, with Danko and Robbie Robertson sharing a mike, early Beatles style, on the harmonies.

At 12:12 A.M., it was over. A fan with a bouquet of a dozen red roses positioned herself in the front row, ready to proffer. "Thank you!" Dylan shouted to the stomping madness. "On behalf of the Band, I want to say thank you, good night!" Danko patted him on the back, and they split.

The roses were left untaken.

At 12:30, one final get-together took place, all the celebrities crowding up the Forum Club, toting glasses and praising Dylan and the Band. Dylan made a quick visit; Robbie Robertson acknowledged the difference between the last show and all the ones previous. "We felt *great* up there," he said, "knowing we were coming onto the end, and that we had done it.

"Yes, we're very tired. With me, it's not my voice, but my fingers." Robertson, who usually stays away from pop gatherings, looked over the crowd—movie stars, pop stars, record producers, company presidents, clustered together in minor constellations, waiters scurrying about filling drink orders.

"So this," said Robbie, "is Hollywood!"

And, around 2 A.M., the true final gathering took place at the Beverly Wilshire hotel, set in the heart of Beverly Hills.

This time around, no stars. Just Dylan with his quiet wife Sara, Robbie Robertson, David Blue, Bobby Neuwirth, Lou Kemp, Dylan's Minnesota boyhood friend, and a few others. Kemp, who still lives and works in Duluth, Minnesota, had been on the entire tour, keeping Dylan company and protecting Dylan's privacy with a Ziegler-like zipper-lip zeal. Between shows in Oakland I asked him about the 36 shows he'd seen so far. Did any of them particularly stand out?

"I'd rather not say."

I heard the matinee show in New York had been outstanding.

"Well . . . they've all been good."

So it was a very private party, a restful farewell to what, on backstage passes, was called Tour '74, and it lasted past four in the morning, the men in the band feeling free. They were finally out of their job and headed for a rest at their homes in nearby Malibu.

Bill Graham was in and out of the Beverly Wilshire suite that morning, a part of the party but, as he did throughout the tour, maintaining what he saw as a respectful distance.

A week later, he was back in his San Francisco office, on the phone again, dealing with Premier Talent Agency for Black Oak Arkansas, Spooky Tooth, King Crimson and Mott the Hoople for Winterland dates.

Graham and FM Productions moved last year out of the Fillmore West building, into a roomy building in midtown San Francisco, at one tip of the industrial sector. Graham's office is modest, modern furniture on light creme carpeting. The walls are filled with photos and gold records and a huge county-town map of the US, all the Dylan/Band stops marked with little paper flags. Near the door is a framed letter from Elvis Presley's manager, signed "The Colonel." Tom Parker had sent an "energy lamp" for Graham and Dylan's use, "to light your way in '74," along with the best from Elvis for the upcoming tour.

And beside Graham is his briefcase, stickered with the logos of the Grateful Dead and the Stones, along with a bumperstrip issued a couple of years ago by David Geffen, chairman of Elektra/Asylum Records, asking: WHO IS DAVID GEFFEN AND WHY IS HE SAYING THOSE TERRIBLE THINGS ABOUT ME?

Geffen and Graham did not appear to get along particularly well on the tour. Now, Geffen was at the peak of his lightning-quick trip to the top of the record business, celebrating his 31st birthday February 21st with the news that his three most recent album releases—Dylan, Joni Mitchell and Carly Simon—were all in the Top Ten, and with a profile piece in Time. Geffen is quoted: " 'The record business is the only part of show business where names are still important. It's still the star system. And this is one of the few places in show business where an executive like me can be a star, too.' "

Geffen also made the cover of Movie Mirror magazine, out the same week Sonny Bono filed for divorce from Cher. The headline, with an arrow pointing to the photo of Geffen, read: CHER IS RUSHING INTO MARRIAGE WITH THIS MAN! Geffen, between parties and other celebrations, could not be reached for comment.

Bill Graham, meantime, is not thinking about Geffen. "I'm full of superlatives," he said. "It's not that I'm hiding negatives; it's that I don't have anything negative to say."

Graham recalled most of the stops on the tour: "Denver was great," he said. (Dylan apparently felt the planet waves and declared from the stage: "It's a full moon!") "The second show," Graham continued, "they were super-energetic, and I don't mean they just yelled and screamed. They were very attentive. It was like the last audience at Fillmore East, people who really came to listen to the music. It didn't feel like 12,000 people. It was like a hootenanny. They really let it out verbally at the end of the songs, and the Band, when they finished the first half, they finished with 'Cripple Creek.' It was just this tumultuous ovation. Very seldom was the reaction out of kilter in relation to the quality of the music that night. And that says something about the audience that Dylan and the Band drew. They drew, I think, a very knowledgeable audience. And I think a lot of people who came to revere didn't revere; they listened.

"Seattle," he continued, "was the only place other than Miami that was festival seating [no reserved seats], which means the earlier you get there the closer you're going to get to the stage, but the people were very orderly, very friendly. Montreal, the energy there was great. Boston . . . a very attentive audience. In Houston, great response. We played a little football with the students once we set up the stage, outside in the soggy grass." A ticket controversy dampened the Ann Arbor concerts at the University of Michigan's Crisler Arena; the local promoter, Bob Begaris, was accused of holding off a block of choice, arena-floor tickets that ended up selling for up to $100. Graham called Begaris "a good promoter, a good friend. Because it was a college campus we didn't do mail-order, and supposedly X amount of tickets—I'd say 500—were held back for VIP treatment, and a scalper got hold of them. I haven't gotten to the bottom of that yet."

The Madison Square Garden concerts—aside from another ticket mess—gave Graham his "nonmusic high" for the tour: "I'd never produced a show in the Garden and I know what the cost of union men is. The union can strangle this town. In many large buildings they make it almost impossible to be creative. They have a reputation for being hard, by-the-book.

"The beginning of the day was almost 'the fastest gun in the West': 'We're the fastest guns in the East. You have to prove yourself to me before I prove myself to you.' And I suggested, 'Let's relax and enjoy the day. Let's get along. Let's play ball. You guys play ball?' And they said, 'Yeah, we play ball.' "

Graham had a backstage storage area cleared out and set up a basketball half-court, out of a forklift, pipes and masking tape. "And they got four guys and it was early in the day and we had a couple of games, and they said, 'Holy shit! This is great. We won't have to hang around and listen to that goddamned rock & roll.' And the foreman, when we left, he said, 'Hey, Billy, we got to have this in our contracts from now on.' They saw that we weren't just hippies earning money on the road with rock & roll freaks. It mellowed everything out. It wasn't 'We love one another,' but for two days we got along. We got along because they respected us as people. And for New York it was a great feeling."

In Oakland, Dylan and the Band had shows at 6 and 10 P.M. and seemed to hurry through the first show, starting only eight minutes past six, skipping the usual half-hour wait, and, altogether, trimming the normal two-and-a-half-hour show by some ten minutes. Dylan looked particularly defiant, having mastered a head-down, eyes-glaring-up posture. "Isn't he wearing eyeliner and pancake make-up?" one woman noticed through binoculars. (He was; a make-up artist was found on each stop to treat Dylan's face.) And in "Wedding Song," Dylan spat out the phrase, "The past is gone," spit showering his microphone.

Dylan seemed looser for the second show. In the audience was the San Francisco pop scene, members of the Grateful Dead, Santana, the Airplane and the Doobie Brothers, along with the dread, full staff from the home office of ROLLING STONE. On the first number, "Most Likely You'll Go Your Way (I'll Go Mine)," he broke a string, smiled, and, after the song, roared into the mike: "Back in San Francisco—at last!"

In San Francisco, Graham took Dylan and the Band on a visit through his warehouse district offices, then up to Marin County, where he showed them his home in Mill Valley and took them to the original dockside restaurant in Sausalito, the Trident, where they stayed two hours past the midnight closing.

In the Bay Area, Graham also helped prevent Dylan from seeing an open letter to Dylan, written by Mimi Farina, singer (and sister of Joan Baez). Published in the San Francisco Chronicle two days before the group's arrival, the letter questioned Dylan about a rumor that had followed his entire tour. The rumor was that Dylan was sending part of his tour profits—Dylan is reported to be getting between 50 and 60% of the expected $3-million net—to Israel to aid in the Mideast war. Another rumor had Dylan sending money to a kibbutz in Israel, for the purchase of food and clothing.

Dylan, in the few interviews he gave during the tour, either denied the rumor or side-stepped the question. He responded to one reporter's question: "That's like asking if I'm doing this tour to raise money to go to the moon in 1983." He told ROLLING STONE (February 14th) the rumors were "just gossip."

Farina, who works with her sister, a founder of the Institute for the Study of Nonviolence, was married to the late Richard Farina, musician and novelist who had been a friend of Dylan in the early Sixties in New York. In her letter she said she doubted the rumors, partly "because of your compassionate understanding for those who suffer." But, she wrote, "The money you earn is the money we are willing to give you . . . if it is going to support the taking of more lives, we should know that before we buy our tickets. Perhaps the question could be clarified by a statement to the press."

Joan Baez said she approved of the letter, but added: "I don't know if it's even our business. But when there's that much money involved, there are bound to be questions."

Mimi did attend an Oakland concert—as Joan's guest—and had an ambivalent response.

"I was glad to see him," she said. "I had dreams later surrounding the concerts. But I wished he'd have communicated more with the audience. Most people were satisfied with the music, but it bothered me that someone with so much power would flippantly ignore it. There was a branch of that old nastiness coming through, by the intonation of his voice. It was snarly, a put-down, even, in tone.

"I brought Kleenex with me. I was ready to cry. But I never had an inkling of emotion, of the poetry behind the songs."

In a national audience of just less than 658,000, Mimi's was a minority voice. Despite the ticket hassles, some obstructed views for several hundred customers in several cities, and an unanswered political question, TOUR '74 was a triumph for Bob Dylan, the Band, the producers, the crews and the audiences. If you didn't have expectations left over from the last time you saw Dylan, eight or 13 years ago; if you could give the man room to do what he wished with his songs—songs that changed the direction of popular music so many times; if you could stand inside his shoes for just one moment, you would have been a satisfied customer. I remember the young girl in Oakland, a Joni Mitchell-like beauty in long jean-skirt outfit, standing with her hands clasped as if in prayer, while the rest of the Coliseum went crazy.

Graham was watching the audiences, too. "You could say, 'greatest thrill of my life,' 'greatest event.' You can't say those things. But it was the kind of thing . . . years from now you remember that picnic; that game where we beat Notre Dame . . . a very special cluster of events that will be with a lot of people. If I don't ever do anything again, I will have thought that I was a part of something very special.

"It's those faces at the end. Those beautiful faces."

Transcript of the Interview with Bob Dylan

By Ben Fong-Torres

(The interview was conducted
January 12th in Dylan's room
at the Chateau Champlain hotel in Montreal.)

Q: You seem to respond to the audiences in your selection of material. In the first show in Chicago you began with "Hero Blues," which wasn't familiar to a lot of the audience, and you and the Band took turns on songs. Now you're doing six straight . . . standards to begin with. How do you decide what songs to do each show?

A: Well, it's more interesting for me to be able to move things around. We chose songs that were important for us, for me, for people we knew. They're mostly the songs that've been recorded through the years.

Q: You haven't done any from *Self-Portrait* so far.

A: I didn't live with those songs for too long. Those were just scraped together.

Q: To, say, make a point or pay tribute to songwriters you liked?

A: Yes.

Q: What about the *Dylan* album? I've heard the songs were mostly outtakes from the *Self-Portrait* sessions.

A: They were just not to be used. I thought it was well understood. They were just to warm up for a tune.

Q: Does Columbia have much more such material?

A: Columbia has a lot of outtakes, but most of them have been bootlegged, I think. [Pause, returning to the *Dylan* album:] I didn't think it was that bad, really! [Laughs]

Q: "Rolling Stone" seems to stand out in the shows as a song that's celebrated more than listened to, and you seem to go along with that response.

A: It's just as real today as it was then. The audience is reacting the same as back then. It was always the one that got the best reaction.

Q: "Rolling Stone" is the finale, and you seem to have begun using "You Go Your Way (I'll Go Mine)" as both opener and final encore. Any special reason?

A: "You Go Your Way" completes a circle in some way.

Q: The tour seemed to get looser as it got to Canada. There was even mention of you on a station in Toronto that more or less claimed you as a Canadian citizen—or at least a man from the north country of the U.S., close to Canada.

A: Canada seems to bridge a gap between the United States and Europe—and England. It's a certain flair. And this is where I come from, this kind of setting—lakes and boats and bridges. [Looks out the hotel-room window at the snowy scenery]

Q: I heard you've been reading the reviews on the shows so far, and several of them seemed disappointed at you for not . . . reaching out more to the audiences. They say you won't say anything and don't seem willing to respond to the emotional receptions you're getting.

A: They just don't understand. It's got nothing to do with that kind of atmosphere. What they [the critics] expect is what they expect. It concerns me more with getting it to the people. It's basically music, not a music-hall routine.

Q: Some people also wondered why you're playing such huge places.

A: I let other people decide that. I just let people know I was ready. Put it in Bill Graham's hands. Originally I wanted to play small halls, but I was just talked out of that.

Q: Is this new activity on your part timed at all? I mean, people sense a *significance* to your returning at this time, given the state of the music business and the state of the country.

A: Well, it wasn't planned . . . I saw daylight; I took off.

Q: Over the past seven or eight years, did you miss being on stage?

A: Sure. There's always those butterflies at a certain point, but then there's the realization that the songs I'm singing mean as much to the people as to me, so it's just up to me to perform the best I can.

Q: You've said that you weren't a spokesman, that "that's in the past." Now you're singing the "message" songs again. Why, and what do you feel, singing the protest songs now?

A: For me, it's just reinforcing those images in my head that were there, that don't die, that will be there tomorrow, and in doing so for myself, hopefully also for those people.

Q: You told me the other night that you were especially looking forward to being in Texas. Why?

A: They're more receptive to my kind of music, my kind of style. In the old days . . . I hate to call them the old days [laughs], I did New York, San Francisco and Austin. The rest were hard in coming. Maybe it's just the Mexican influence.

Q: Will you play in Mexico someday?

A: I wanted to play Mexico, but it was hard to reroute the whole tour. I also want to play South America sometime.

Q: You made a reference to astrology in explaining—in *Newsweek*—why you were back on the road. ["Saturn has been an obstacle in my planetary system. It's been there for the last few ages and just removed itself from my system. I feel free and unburdened."] What's your interest in astrology?

A: I can't read anybody's chart, but the thing about Saturn is, I didn't know what it was at the time or I would've gone somewhere away. It's a big, heavy obstacle that comes into your chain of events, that fucks you up in a big way. Came into my chart a few years ago and just flew off again a couple of months ago.

Q: Who told you about Saturn's existence?

A: Someone very dear to me told me.

Q: Is Malibu pretty much your home now?

A: We're just there temporarily. It was cold in New York and we didn't want to go back there after Mexico. I can't stay away from New York!

Q: You've done six concerts now and your voice seems to be holding up pretty well.

A: We've been through the big tours before. Actually, I'd like to have a little club where I could go and sing when I felt like it.

Q: Why does your voice change so much? From the country albums to *Pat Garrett and Billy the Kid* to the way you sound on tour. . . .

A: [Reflective pause] . . . That's a good question. I don't know. I could only guess, if it *has* changed. I've never gone for having a great voice, for cultivating one. I'm still not doing it now.

Q: Maybe people say your voice has changed because of your reworking or rearranging well-known songs like "Lay Lady Lay."

A: You'll always stretch things out or cut it up, just to keep interested. If you can't stay interested that way, you'll have to lose track. But I'm me now. That's the way it comes out.

Q: You're meaner now?

A: Yeah.

Q: How are you meaner these days?

A: Oh—no, I said, "I'm me now."

Q: Well! I already had the headline made up: "Dylan beats kids. 'I'm meaner now!' "

I'd like to ask you about the rumors about your giving some of the profits from this tour to the Israeli war effort. One rumor has it that you're sending money in your father's name, and you've been characterized as an "ultra-Zionist."

A: I'm not sure what a Zionist really is. I don't know how those things get started, really. It's just gossip.

Q: Maybe so, but people do wonder about what religion means to you.

A: Religion to me is a fleeting thing. Can't nail it down. It's in me and out of me.

Q: But it seems to be "in" you enough for religious images to become parts of your songs.

A: It does give me, on the surface, some images, but I don't know to what degree. Like Da Vinci going in to paint the Last Supper. Until he finishes it, no one knows what the Last Supper is. He goes out and finds 12 guys, puts them around this table, and there's your Last Supper. Or Moses. He found a guy and painted him, and forever, that guy will be Moses. But why Moses or the Last Supper? Why not a flower? Or a tree?

Q: Aside from religion, people talk about how you're now a family man, how you've mellowed out, and how all that has affected your music.

A: Yeah, to a degree. But those things don't make a person settle down. A family brings the world together. You can see it's all one. Paints a better picture than being with a chick and traveling all over the world or hanging out all night. [Phone rings; Dylan answers, talks for a few seconds and hangs up.] But I still get that spark. Fame threw me for a loop at first. Until I learned how to swim with it and until I learned to turn it around—so you can just throw it in the closet and pick it up when you need it. . . . I'm still out there. In no way am I not. I don't live on a pedestal.

Q: When did you learn to turn it around?

A: The turning point was back in Woodstock. A little after the accident. Sitting around one night under a full moon, looked out into the bleak woods and I said, "Something's gotta change."

There was some business that had to be taken care of that we don't have to go into. But it was too much. It finally broke the camel's back. Now it's the same old me again.

Q: In *Pat Garrett and Billy the Kid,* do you think that you pretty much played the role of Dylan?

A: I don't know who I played. I tried to play whoever it was in the story, but I guess it's a known fact that there was nobody in that story that was the character I played.

Q: Would you like to be a movie star?

A: I'm not a movie star, but I've got a vision to put up on the screen. Someday we'll get around to doing it. The Peckinpah experience was valuable in terms of getting near the big action.

Q: Will you do a couple of films on your own before producing the "vision"?

A: The Peckinpah movie brought me as close as I'll get. I've been on sets of movies and TV shows, but they were small-time compared. They spent $4, $5 million on *Billy the Kid,* had all the top people. So that was really heavy. Gave me that vibration. When I finally do mine, it'll have that vibration.

Q: How'd you happen to get involved in *Billy the Kid?*

A: Just one thing into another. [Pause] They took me on because I was a big name.

Q: How'd you feel, seeing the rushes of your scenes?

A: I've seen myself on screen [*Don't Look Back, Eat the Document*]. Movies don't impress me. That part didn't scare me off at all. Just hoped I didn't get shot during the movie!

Q: What about Ashes and Sand, the label you were starting yourself?

A: It only lasted a quick few minutes.

Q: Whose idea was it for you to have your own label?

A: I advised myself it was a good thing, and then I advised myself that it wasn't. I just didn't need it.

Q: You were going to sign new artists. I hear you're interested in Leon Redbone, that you talked with his agent in Toronto.

A: Leon interests me. I've heard he's anywhere from

25 to 60. I've been this close [indicates a foot] to him, and I can't tell. If I had a label I'd want him. He does old Jimmy Rodgers, then turns around and does a Robert Johnson.

Q: Who else have you seen that you like?

A: A couple of guys in Chicago were good—Mickey Clark and another Mickey.

Q: You told *Newsweek* that there's a new generation, that "everybody's thinking the same thing." Basically, that this isn't a time when we need protest songs. I was talking to a member of the Committee back in San Francisco who said there's still a need to get people to come around, that someone out there elected Nixon again after four years and continues to support him, through Watergate. Do you really believe that "everybody's thinking the same thing" and that you no longer need to write "message" songs?

A: There's still a message. But the same electric spark that went off back then could still go off again—the spark that led to nothing. Our kids will probably protest, too. Protest is an old thing. Sometimes protest is deeper or different—the Haymarket Square or the Russian Revolution. The Civil War, that's protest. There's always a need for protest songs. You just gotta tap it.

Q: What did you think of CBS firing Clive Davis?

A: I thought he was a scapegoat.

Q: He was trying to re-sign you when he left. If he were still at Columbia, might you have signed with them again?

A: He would've made no difference.

Q: Why did you leave CBS?

A: It was long overdue. Just a feeling it was time to go on. A gut feeling. Suspected they were doing more talk than action. Just released 'em and that's all. Got a feeling they didn't care whether I stayed there or not.

Q: Why did you choose to go with David Geffen and Asylum Records?

A: He's there. Columbia's not there.

Q: What's "there"?

A: Whatever it takes to be there.

Q: Are you actually signed, by contract, to Asylum?

A: I'm not so sure we signed one. I don't sign anything these days.

Q: What about your work with Leon Russell? You did only a couple of things with him.

A: The producers that have meant the most to me are Tom Wilson, John Hammond, and Bob Johnston. They were there. They were there when . . . well, it's like a small group of friends. Leon and I, we didn't do that much. [Dylan couldn't remember how many songs they had produced together.] It went fine. It was as good as it could've been expected to be.

THE PRESS REVIEWS THE TOUR

Dylan: The Times Are A-Changin' Again

By Nat Hentoff

On the color set, "old blue eyes" was very much on—Frank Sinatra, puffy, bathed in light, back on stage in Las Vegas, the last fragment of his "retirement" dissolved. Coming into the room, my 12-year-old son watched for a few seconds, and asked, "Is that Bob Dylan?"

I mention this to put the Resurrection of Bob Dylan in a somewhat longer time perspective than has been evident in the reams of copy about the current national tour by the kid from Minnesota. (Or as Bing Crosby, trying to stop a fight in a bar, once said to the contestants, "Come on, what's it all going to mean a hundred years from now?" Bing was lucky to get out alive that night.)

This is not to say that Dylan's impact won't be felt for a long time. A professor of political science at the University of Massachusetts is conducting an investigation, by questionnaire, to try to identify the "major agents of change during the 1960's"; and Bob Dylan's name has been on many of the lists he's been getting back, including mine.

Dylan was Isaiah in a corduroy cap, calling down the

hard rain. Lyrics from his songs were on the walls of student dorms and bathrooms, as well as on placards in antiwar demonstrations. At first he marveled at and enjoyed his ascension as a prophet. Soon, however, he became apprehensive as his songs began to be searched for hidden routes of deliverance. "I'm not part of no Movement," he told me in 1964. "I do a lot of things no Movement would allow."

It was at the end of that conversation that Dylan invited me to Woodstock the next week. "I'll give you a ride on my motorcycle." I never made it; and two years later, he almost didn't, when his cycle smashed both itself and him.

When Dylan recovered, he no longer made himself available to journalists, and then he was unavailable to fans as well—except for such extremely rare public performances as the New York concert to raise money for the homeless in Bangladesh. He also showed up at a tribute to Woody Guthrie who, as Dylan puts it, was his "last idol."

In 1968, Harold Leventhal, manager of a number of singers and actors, and Woody's friend and protector, gave Dylan some books about Israel and finally convinced him to go there. "After his father died," Leventhal told me, "Bob became quite conscious of his Jewishness. He was very excited about Israel when he got back. And it was around that time he started talking with Rabbi Meier Kahane who formed the Jewish Defense League. But before that, Kahane had been Arlo Guthrie's Hebrew teacher. Small world, huh?"

During the Yom Kippur War, Leventhal tried to organize a big benefit concert for Israel at Madison Square Garden. He asked Dylan to perform, but Dylan declined. "Later," Leventhal says, "I found out that Bob had given a sizable amount of money to Israel."

I had seen Dylan only to wave to in the Village in recent years, but mutual friends who had spent some time with him reported that although he had certainly found a center of gravity in his wife and family and, in a way, in his sense of himself as a Jew, Dylan was getting restless. As garishly costumed and often bizarre "glitter rock" (or, as Steve Stills calls it, "creep rock") attracted larger and increasingly corybantic audiences, Dylan wondered whether he could still make contact—"live"—through his music. There was also that competitive drive I saw in him when he was a scruffy kid, asking Mike Porco if he could sing once in a while at Gerde's Folk City, which Porco still owns. Dylan-the-kid was not uninterested in fame.

Oddly, however, even after he had more than arrived in the mid-1960's, Dylan's recordings never sold in as huge quantities as those of the Beatles, the Rolling Stones, and even that strident group of permanent beginners which calls itself Chicago. Could he fuse a return tour (the first in eight years) with a new album (*Planet Waves* on Asylum) to create a take which would top his best years of the last decade?

That question has already been answered to Dylan's satisfaction. He has also revealed, by the way, a business acumen which more performers ought to be acquiring. Dylan's arrangement with Asylum brings him royalties of at least 80 cents a record (I think it's more, but nobody's talking for the record). Dylan received no advance money but, with one of the biggest slices of the profits any record star has ever gotten, he didn't need an advance. And having the money stretched out also has tax benefits.

Soon after *Planet Waves* was officially released, it was certified "gold" (sales of a million dollars) by the Recording Industry Association of America. "Hell," an old friend in the record business told me the morning after Dylan's first Madison Square Garden concert on January 30, "if there were such a thing, that album could soon be certified 'platinum.' "

At that first New York concert, there was no question that most of the crowd (largely in their twenties, but ranging from such teen-agers as John Kennedy, Jr. to graybearded oldsters and the—uh—ageless Yoko Ono) felt they were part of a *musical,* not only a media event. My own reaction was mixed. Dylan, returned, sings with greater authority and somewhat more depth and variety of texture than he did during his first glory years, but he didn't quite turn me on.

Part of the problem was the sound system which frequently made the lyrics aş opaque as a newly discovered Dead Sea scroll. "The excitement of the evening," Harold Leventhal said in his customary kindly way, "made up for what one couldn't penetrate." (For future reference, the only way, an imperfect one, to cope with transmogrified acoustics in a large auditorium is to cup your ear with your hand, a device I learned from years of broadcasting football games and track meets from an open booth.)

But the splintered sound was not the only explanation for my conviction that the Band, which accompanied Dylan, is far more stimulating than he. Even at its best, Dylan's voice is a decidedly limited instrument. When he was riding the zeitgeist in the 1960's, however, it didn't much matter what he sounded like. It was his passion, energy, anger, and vulnerability that came through so affectingly. It was seeing and hearing the rebel kid not only making it, but starkly proclaiming—as he regularly does again on this tour—that a time inexorably comes when even the President of the United States "must stand naked."

In those swirling years, Dylan was, as the Quakers say, speaking truth to power, even if the words were occasionally Delphic. ("Something is happening, but you don't know what it is, do you, Mr. Jones?") The times they are a-changin' again, and the nation once more is ripe for a rocking Isaiah; but Dylan's sound and beat are of the past. Some performers certainly do transcend time barriers—the best jazz and country musicians and singers always have. But other styles become period pieces. The sound is retrospectively interesting, particularly if it's coming from a living legend, but there is a lack of musical fulfillment for right now.

The Band, on the other hand, while uneven in the past, is now perhaps the most exhilaratingly "together" group in all of country rock. The rural churchlike vocal harmonies thrusting out into space like spears; the hard but loose percussion; the joyously unabashed honky-tonk piano; the careening interstitching instrumental skills of all these raffish minstrels; and above all, the Band's beat, are true phenomena. They stretch time, curve it around corners, lash it and caress it, all the while keeping up a whirlpool-like pulsation that almost had me up and dancing, and I don't dance no steps of any era.

If the Band, which considered its opening New York performance only "mildly okay," can sustain this level of collective celebration, its performances will never be dated —just as Eddie "Cleanhead" Vinson will be fundamentally contemporary so long as he blows his alto and sings his crackling blues.

What it comes down to, I'm afraid, is that Dylan, now as then, is an undistinguished musician, vocally and instrumentally. His lyrics, then and sometimes now, are provocatively arresting; but as performed by Dylan at the age of 32 in 1974, the gestalt is anachronistic. It may well be that for some years to come, Bob Dylan will attract even huger audiences than welcomed him back on this tour, but most of them will be following old cue cards. There's nothing wrong with that. I feel that way about Tom Wolfe (the novelist, not the cute fellow in the white suit). I am not likely to pick up *Look Homeward, Angel* these days, but I sure am grateful for the goat cries and the train-sounds of the American night that Wolfe put into my head when I was in my teens.

You can only go home for a visit, unless you've stopped growing, and that's how Dylan's return strikes me.

"He's not 'The Kid' any more," my wife said as we were leaving the Garden. "So what can he be now?"

What Dylan is now, on the other hand, is a most considerate man. He made sure that opening night tickets were sent to Marjorie Guthrie, Woody's widow; and to Bob and Sidsel Gleason, at whose New Jersey home Dylan would visit Woody during the periods Woody was allowed out of the hospital, before he couldn't move at all. Also on Dylan's list of tickets was Mike Porco, who gave the kid his first chance in the Big Apple.

To my surprise, I was on that list too. I was touched, and still am. Dylan put me on that list before he knew I was going to write anything about this tour, and I am sorry I can't be more enthusiastic. But I did like that trip back, Bob, and I'm glad you've found a real-life home to stay, not just for passing through.

Bob Dylan Comes Back from the Edge

By Lucian K. Truscott, IV

Wandering through the crowd during intermission at The Concert last Wednesday night, one got a sense of why it must have been an agonizing decision for Bob Dylan to go on tour for the first time in eight years, of why the Big Apple has been dreaded as much as looked forward to. Old friends of Dylan were there, and so were many who remember him from basket houses on MacDougal Street and Gerde's Folk City over 10 years ago.

The things Dylan must like about New York City—he has mentioned it in nearly every interview he has given—were here to haunt him as well as help him. He can walk through the Village without being noticed, and if he is recognized, no one makes a big deal out of it. He can jam with John Prine at the Bitter End without being mobbed or driven crazy by autograph-glommers or teenyboppers. Here he can raise a family in the same old tension and peace and quiet and noise of the city which gave him the images and experiences for songs like "Visions of Johanna," "Mr. Tambourine Man," and "Like a Rolling Stone."

But the peculiar schizophrenia of stardom has a way of coming back around like a death-dealing boomerang. The city that ignores Bob Dylan on the street is perfectly capable of leaving him equally high and dry on a stage. And though that did not happen on Wednesday night—he had the crowd on its feet, screaming, stomping, and clapping at the end—there were those among his friends and long-time admirers, among those who hold him most dearly, who were, if not disappointed, at least a bit deflated after their first evening in years with Bob Dylan. It was great to see him again, but the years had taken their toll. There was something missing—maybe in us, maybe in Dylan—and no one knew exactly what it was.

Dylan said, "I'm honored to be here," and sang six classics: "Everybody *must* get stoned" drew screams and more lighted joints from an already grass-soaked audience.

Yet Dylan's stage fright, as the Band reminded us in its first solo number, was painfully evident. "Lay Lady Lay," which reviews of the Chicago and Philadelphia concerts have described as taking on the old "Dylan Edge," was simply rushed, hurried through and cast off like the last tune in a long, tedious rehearsal. Dylan was scared. What appeared at first to be new sparkles and flourishes on a laid-back country song was really his nervousness showing through.

Dylan attacked the mike, his brow furrowed, mouth working madly from side to side, and "It Ain't Me, Babe" was coughed out between gritted teeth. On "Ballad of a Thin Man," Dylan's insistent, pounding grand piano work rushed the song to the point of impatience. Garth Hudson's organ fills disappeared in a bad sound mix. Dylan rose up and banged down, running wildly along the keyboard, driving the Band brilliantly, forcefully, but just too goddam fast.

But it was on "Just Like Tom Thumb's Blues" that whatever was bothering Dylan came through most clearly. The song is a beautiful one, ablaze with painful autobiographical images and self-exploration. On record, Dylan's voice searches its way through the lyrics, finding one color here, another there. The emotional content of the song is as much in the way Dylan sang it—in the depths of his voice—as in the depth of the words. And listening to the song as I write this, I am reminded that Dylan's magic was in large part this: the mix of lyrics and vocal coloration. The galaxy of emotions he could plumb between the boundaries of one song was greater than any rock and roll artist who came before him or has come along since. His voice is truly one of the great rock and roll instruments.

On Wednesday night, the song was rushed through, along with the others, so much chaff to be brushed aside in search of solitude. Dylan struck a pose—tough, defiant, almost mean in its intensity—and sang without searching. His emphasis—or was it reliance—on highs permeated the song. He would raise a verse to a fever pitch, drop it, then raise another, screaming into the mike. He gazed above the heads of the crowd, intent and serious, then he'd back off. It was automatic, studied. Dylan wouldn't let the song carry him as much as he carried the song. He refused to search back through the lyrics for the experiences and feelings which gave it birth, allowing him to bring it back to life again.

Dylan was afraid, that was for sure. But "Just Like Tom Thumb's Blues" showed he wasn't afraid of us, the audience. It was himself he feared—the process of going back over those songs which bore the pain of becoming Bob Dylan, the highs, the lows, all of that life which was *living on the edge*. He seemed unwilling to go through it all again in song, dredging up that which was better off left behind. The funny thing was, one could hardly blame him.

The Band played alone to a warm reception, and then Dylan returned to sing "All Along the Watchtower," "The Ballad of Hollis Brown," and "Knockin' on Heaven's Door." He wore a black tuxedo and a silver and black ruffled cowboy shirt. The trousers of the tux hung loosely —almost baggy—giving him the appearance of a young Charlie Chaplin, legs spread wide, elegant in his awkwardness.

After intermission, Dylan returned alone to sing five

acoustic numbers. "The Times They Are A-Changin' " ran fast, and brilliantly embellished harmonica breaks drew extended applause. "Don't Think Twice It's All Right," and then "Gates of Eden." Like "Tom Thumb," the latter was sung with an intensity which bordered on anxiousness. My notes made toward the end of the song read: "What made song great on record—he was calling on something w/in him, bringing it out. . . . in performance he leans on drama . . . teeth gritted, lips contorting 2-3 times on one vowel, bitten off . . . overdramatized."

"Just Like a Woman" followed, and it was sung slower, more confidently. "It's Alright, Ma (I'm Only Bleeding)" was done with lovely, hypnotic speed, sung up and out and proud and sane. It seemed that Dylan had hit a stride, that he had found his voice, a way to cope with standing naked before 20,000 pairs of eyes. "It's Alright, Ma" was markedly different from the original, but for the first time all night I had the sense that the song had grown, not shrunk. Dylan's comfort came through nobly, he dropped his tough front, and even in the clippedy clip way he ran down the words one could feel him feeling his way, wringing the song, and himself, almost dry. He must have felt good, because he swaggered a bit when he took his bows, lifting his hands in a triumphant wave.

The Band came on again for several numbers. They took no chances with the crowd. Every song sounded just like the record, and they sustained the tension of each song right up until the last chord. The tone of Richard Manuel's voice, I have in my notes, was "precise and coarse, as opposed to Dylan—changing, unpredictable, solitary, weird."

Dylan returned and ran through a slow version of "Forever Young," from his new album, as well as "Something There Is About You." Then he and the Band broke into "Like a Rolling Stone," the lights came up, and all hell broke loose, kids in the aisles, all the magic and madness of one of the all-time great rock and roll songs. They didn't rush the song, but didn't loaf either. It came off perfectly, a real New York song bringing back everything the crowd had come to hear: all about innocence and discovery, self-imposed hardship and coping, a romantic vision of a romantic period in the lives of many in the crowd. Jesus, it was great.

Dylan's appeal was always, and still is, to the white middle class. The concert crowd came dressed shabbily, elegantly, all the ways that people who can afford the choice turn themselves out. They lit up $40-an-ounce grass, snorted coke, flashed gold rings and fancy boots, wore pre-faded jeans and expensive Indian jewelry, snapped pictures with the most expensive photographic equipment money can buy. Any Dylan fan who griped about the $9.50 high ticket, or who called on millionaire Bob for a "free" concert is guilty of not having listened to the songs they were screaming for all night. For the songs of Bob Dylan are thick with all the contradictions, all the weirdness and schizophrenia of growing up middle-class, of looking for romance in poverty, on the highway, or bumming around and returning to from whence he (and they) came.

Dylan told Rolling Stone magazine, "Now it's the me again." If there is one thing true about Bob Dylan over the years, it's that he is in never-ending state of flux. There is no new Dylan or old Dylan or country Dylan or Edge Dylan. There is simply Dylan, and listening to him live gives one some idea of the dimensions of his brilliance, fallibility, strength, weakness, pain, and triumphs. He has been constantly growing and expanding, just as he grew in concert from a faulty, uncertain start to an incredible, fiery end. If he at times disappoints his critics, he never has ceased to amaze them.

And finally, watching and listening to Dylan the other night—and on records since then—has made me realize how desperately we want our heroes to be self-destructive, as if only by living recklessly can they show us their essential humanity, their impermanence and mortality. I remember when *Nashville Skyline* and *Self-Portrait* were released, how the critics and the fans seized on them to prove that Dylan's long absence from the scene, his retreat to Woodstock, had mellowed him out, left him without the old edge he showed in *Blonde on Blonde* or *Highway 61 Revisited.* God, how they moaned and groaned, as if Dylan had somehow deserted, never to return. Here was Dylan singing country—which had roots in racism and bigotry, the critics chanted. And here was Dylan on *Self-Portrait* rhyming "moon" with "June." All of it was inexcusable, without redeeming value. Where was the old Dylan, with his moral lefts and protest rights, his haunting images and incisive social criticism?

It's an old story. We read about Zelda and Fitzgerald now, and shake our heads and say, Christ, what a shame, but what a life they led! And we read about Jackson Pollock, and shake our heads and say, gee, too bad about his drinking and his craziness, but look at all the fantastic art he produced! Now the same sort of head-shaking and tongue-clucking appreciation is being shown for Jimi Hendrix and Janis Joplin. One figures everyone would be more happy with Dylan's extensive, if uneven, body of work if he, too, were dead. Then we couldn't lean back, turn up the volume, and talk among ourselves about all the speed and acid he must have done, back in the days when he wrote the songs we remember him best for.

Well, life sometimes doesn't work out that way. Despite the morbidity of hero worship, our expectation is that the great should live up to our worst fantasies and best lies. Bob Dylan has simply settled down with a wife and kids. He eats vegetables. He drinks wine. By all counts, he dotes on the goodness and wholeness of family life. In his most recent songs, he appears to thank his wife for saving his life.

One can hardly blame Dylan for having opted for life, for having quit his life out there on the Edge—all the late-night craziness and running around, the terrible manic existence he is said to have had before his motorcycle accident. On Wednesday night, he seemed skittish of the past which stares him in the face every time he runs back through the stark chronicle of his life in song. And so some of those songs were performed, not sung.

"But who can blame him?" said one old friend of his. "At least he took his chances, pushing things, letting it go.

The Band just did their records. Dylan wouldn't settle for that."

So as usual, Bob Dylan is growing in his own way, at his own speed. The songs on his new album, the laid-back celebrations of being a father, life at home, and his ongoing love ballad to his wife, they all seem so calm, so content and full. The craziness, the pain, the weirdness—all are missing. Perhaps someday we'll catch up. And maybe then, we too will stop acting forever young, and have it within us to wish it on someone else.

Dylan and Fans: Looking Back, Going On

By Ellen Willis

A couple of weeks before Bob Dylan's arrival in New York, I got a letter from my friend, colleague, and fellow Dylan freak Greil Marcus, of *Creem.* He was upset about some lyrics from Dylan's new album, *Planet Waves,* that had been previewed in *Newsweek*—they sounded so complacent—and full of the same ambivalences that had been afflicting me with a queasy stomach ever since the tour was announced. Unreconciled to the happy-family-man posture Dylan had adopted since his motorcycle accident, we hoped and doubted. Did he still have the power to move us—to *matter*—as he once had? If so, did he have any intention of using it? And if not, why was he bothering to tour at all—he certainly didn't need the money. The reports from the first cities on his itinerary were inconclusive, and what little I'd heard about *Planet Waves* was not encouraging—it seemed we were in for more domesticity and low-keyed, moderate angst. But then, Dylan's critics had been obtuse before. Not for nothing was he opening and closing concerts with "Most Likely You'll

Go Your Way (I'll Go Mine)": "Time will tell just who has fell, and who's been left behind."

My theory was that Dylan was consciously working against the grain of his genius in order to communicate honestly about his own strategy for survival. In a way (a classically Dylanesque irony), he was only being consistent: *Blonde on Blonde,* it was worth remembering, was almost entirely about coping. It was the context that had changed. The sixties imperative was to strip away psychic defenses and social hypocrisies: through drugs we were to become Adam and Eve; through a politics of personal encounter and confrontation we were to create, *ex nihilo,* the post-revolutionary human being. All over the place, people were dismantling their personalities, giving no more thought to the prospect of having to put the fragments back together than the kid who takes a watch apart to see how it works. And at some point in each person's trip there had to come a moment of decision: plunge ahead, with a high probability of ending up dead or insane—or pull back. Dylan was like the rest of us, only more so. He went farther out than most, and his retrenchment was correspondingly dramatic. Since *John Wesley Harding*—which I now think of as the first seventies album, released at a time when it hadn't even crossed my mind that the sixties were going to end—he had been increasingly preoccupied with putting himself back together and making some sort of peace with the world as it existed. I couldn't fault him for that; in my own way, I was trying to do the same thing. Nor could I justify demanding that Bob Dylan get my kicks for me—or take my risks for me. The only sixties figure that had meant anywhere near as much to me as Dylan was Janis Joplin, and I didn't need a weatherman to know which way *that* wind blew.

The other part of the irony was that Dylan's new direction posed its own risk. Rock in the sixties had a redemptive quality; it put us in touch with our potential. The Beatles brought out our joy, the Stones our sensuality. Dylan's great contribution was to enlarge our capacity for freedom, help us break out of mental and emotional, musical and lyrical boxes. To decide that there was no freedom like chaos, and chaos was no freedom at all, was to relinquish his special gift and become just another—well, not quite *just* another—intelligent and talented songwriter, struggling with the problem of how to make maturity interesting. The risk was not that Dylan would destroy his myth, which was exactly what he intended to do, but that in the process he would lose his old audience without gaining a new one. It occurred to me that Dylan's return to the stage might very well have been calculated to forestall that possibility. If so, it was a characteristically brilliant move. The emergence of the sixties' chief culture hero—possibly for the last time—was bound to attract enormous crowds and maximum publicity. Dylan's performances were giving him a chance to re-establish his ties with old fans and reach thousands of new ones. Perhaps most important in the long run, excitement over the tour had stimulated a huge advance sale for *Planet Waves,* which appeared certain to become Dylan's first No. 1 L.P.

Ultimately, it was this evidence of Dylan's continuing preeminence as a media artist which convinced me that his concerts at Madison Square Garden would be momentous. I was right. The two evening performances were masterpieces of controlled intensity. The first show, in particular, was a catharsis I hadn't even known I needed—a celebration of the past and a going beyond. Dylan performed his old songs almost exclusively, but if he was looking back, it was not to invite but to reject nostalgia. Nostalgia implied revival, which implied death, and it was obvious from the moment the concert began that even Dylan's earliest songs were not only still alive but resonant with new meanings. When the crowd cheered a line like "Even the President of the United States sometimes must have to stand naked," it was reacting less to a fortuitous political reference than to the uncanny adaptability of Dylan's vision. The songs themselves were enough to make the point, but Dylan underscored it with new arrangements—a country-rock "It Ain't Me, Babe," an upbeat "Ballad of a Thin Man," an acoustic "Just Like a Woman." During his acoustic set—the part of the concert I liked least—he did a lot of fooling around with his voice, which occasionally worked but more often strangled songs with excessive volume and heavy-handed, arbitrary phrasing. What he seemed to be saying (at least to me—God knows what all the eighteen-year-olds were thinking!) was that we had been through some very special years. They had shaped us, marked us. They would always be part of us, something that we shared; they still had meaning for our lives. Yet we had to move on. That evening, anyway, Dylan wasn't about to tell us how—it was tact, as well as showmanship, that dictated his repertoire. We would go our way, he would go his, but that didn't mean we couldn't be friends.

Toward the end, after the Band's second set, Dylan did two songs from *Planet Waves*. "Forever Young" was supposedly addressed to his children, but its advice (Dylan never could resist being didactic, even when he was proclaiming that messages were a drag) was obviously meant for us as well: "May you always know the truth and see the light surrounding you. . . . May you have a strong foundation when the winds of changes shift," and, finally, a child-of-the-sixties blessing (or curse) if there ever was one, "May you stay forever young." "Something There Is About You," a love song to his wife, made the only direct comment of the night on Dylan's current state of mind: "I was in a whirlwind, Now I'm in some better place." And then came the big one—"Like a Rolling Stone." It crept up on us—Dylan had changed the intro, of course—and exploded.

"How does it feel?" we screamed.

"How does it feel—to be on your own—no direction home—"

It felt as I would have expected: wonderful. The lights went out; flickering matches transformed the Garden into a giant planetarium. Dylan and the Band came back for a reprise of "Most Likely You'll Go Your Way," left, came back again, and ended with a rousing electric version of "Blowin' in the Wind." I went home as high on Dylan as I'd ever been.

I'm still feeling that way, and in my present mood I can almost psych myself into thinking that *Planet Waves* is a great album. It isn't, but neither is it as inconsequential as those *Newsweek* quotes portended. By now, we ought to know better than to judge Dylan's words on paper; it is his singing that makes the difference. And the singing on *Planet Waves* is fine. The polish of *Nashville Skyline* and *New Morning* has been abandoned in favor of a crude expressiveness that undercuts the lyrical banalities —which on closer inspection often turn out to be not so banal after all. Take "Wedding Song," for instance. "Your love cuts like a knife"? "I love you more than blood"? Not exactly your conventional images of marital bliss. As he often does, Dylan is using clichés, or apparent clichés, to camouflage innovation. Though nobody seems to have noticed, *Planet Waves* is unlike all other Dylan albums: it is openly personal. It could be argued that Dylan's mask has simply become more subtle, but I don't believe it. I think the subject of *Planet Waves* is what it appears to be —Dylan's aesthetic and practical dilemma ("I been walkin' on the road, I been livin' on the edge, Now I just got to go before I get to the ledge") and his immense emotional debt to Sara. The album is dominated by tributes to her. But there is also an anti-love song called "Dirge," whose anti-heroine (success? the audience? Joan Baez? Albert Grossman? Sara's alter ego?) is "a painted face on a trip down suicide road." This kind of symbolism can be embarrassing. Dylan has always tended to get sticky about women—to classify them as goddesses to be idolized or bitches to be mercilessly trashed. Yet his conviction that he has been saved by love is so poignant and so obviously genuine that it transcends the stereotype. Which is, in a sense, what popular culture is all about.

SONGS PERFORMED ON THE TOUR

Dylan Solos

Blowin' in the Wind
Don't Think Twice
Except You
Gates of Eden
Girl from the North Country
It's Alright, Ma
Just Like a Woman
The Lonesome Death of Hattie Carroll
Love Minus Zero
Mama, You've Been on my Mind
Song to Woody
The Times They Are A'Changin'
To Ramona
Wedding Song

Band Solos All Along the Watchtower
Ballad of a Thin Man
Holy Cow
I Don't Believe You
I Shall Be Released
King Harvest
Life's a Carnival
Long Black Veil
Loving You
The Night They Drove Old Dixie Down
Rag Mama Rag
The Shape I'm In
Share Your Love
Stage Fright
This Wheel's on Fire
Up on Cripple Creek
The Weight
When You Awake

Dylan and Band

All Along the Watchtower
As I Went Out One Morning
Ballad of a Thin Man
Forever Young
Hero Blues
Hollis Brown
I Don't Believe You
It Ain't Me, Babe
It Takes Alot To Laugh
Just Like Tom Thumb's Blues
Knockin' on Heaven's Door
Lay Lady Lay
Leopard Skin Pillbox Hat
Like a Rolling Stone
Maggie's Farm
Most Likely You Go Your Way
The Night They Drove Old Dixie Down
Rainy Day Women
Something There Is About You
Stage Fright
Tom Thumb's Blues
Tough Mama